We love your feedback!
If you have any comments or suggestions
on this book, please drop us a line at
AquascapeHobbyBooks@gmail.com.

If you like this book, please consider leaving us
a review on Amazon.

How To Use This Book

Use the "My Tanks" page to list all the tanks you plan to track in this book. Make sure to give each one a unique name or ID. Use that Name/ID on the following pages to identify which tank you're recording information for.

The "Organism Inventory" pages can be used to track when you acquire fish, corals, crustaceans, mollusks, or even plants. We recommend limiting each sheet to one tank for clarity.

The rest of the pages are Maintenance Logs for daily or weekly maintenance. You can record data about the water quality and water changes. Each page also has a handy maintenance checklist, and space for general notes.

My Tanks

Name / ID	Size	Description	Date Started
_____	_____	_____	_____
_____	_____	_____	_____
_____	_____	_____	_____
_____	_____	_____	_____
_____	_____	_____	_____

Organism Inventory

Tank name/ID: _____

Description	Source	Date Added	Date Lost

Organism Inventory

Tank name/ID: _____

Description	Source	Date Added	Date Lost

Organism Inventory

Tank name/ID: _____

Description	Source	Date Added	Date Lost

Organism Inventory

Tank name/ID: _____

Description	Source	Date Added	Date Lost

Organism Inventory

Tank name/ID: _____

Description	Source	Date Added	Date Lost

Organism Inventory

Tank name/ID: _____

Description	Source	Date Added	Date Lost

Organism Inventory

Tank name/ID: _____

Description	Source	Date Added	Date Lost

Organism Inventory

Tank name/ID: _____

Description	Source	Date Added	Date Lost

Organism Inventory
Tank name/ID: _____

Description	Source	Date Added	Date Lost

Organism Inventory

Tank name/ID: _____

Description	Source	Date Added	Date Lost

Organism Inventory

Tank name/ID: _____

Description	Source	Date Added	Date Lost
_____	_____	_____	_____
_____	_____	_____	_____
_____	_____	_____	_____
_____	_____	_____	_____
_____	_____	_____	_____
_____	_____	_____	_____
_____	_____	_____	_____
_____	_____	_____	_____
_____	_____	_____	_____
_____	_____	_____	_____
_____	_____	_____	_____
_____	_____	_____	_____
_____	_____	_____	_____
_____	_____	_____	_____
_____	_____	_____	_____
_____	_____	_____	_____
_____	_____	_____	_____
_____	_____	_____	_____
_____	_____	_____	_____
_____	_____	_____	_____
_____	_____	_____	_____
_____	_____	_____	_____
_____	_____	_____	_____
_____	_____	_____	_____

Organism Inventory

Tank name/ID: _____

Description	Source	Date Added	Date Lost

Maintenance Logs

Date: Tank name/ID:

Data

Water level: _____   Ammonia level: _____

Temperature: _____   Nitrite level: _____

pH level: _____   Nitrate level: _____

Alkalinity: _____   Salinity: _____

Calcium level: _____   Phosphate level: _____

Iodine level: _____   Magnesium level: _____

Cleaning checklist

Water change?   ☐ yes   ☐ no   Amount changed: _____

☐   Glass   ☐   Gravel   ☐   Top   ☐   Other _____

Maintenance Checklist

<u>notes</u>

☐   Filters   ☐ rinse   ☐ replace   _____

☐   Pumps   _____

☐   Tubing   _____

☐   Connections   _____

☐   Airstones   _____

☐   Skimmers, etc.   _____

☐   Lighting   _____

Restock (food, treatments, equipment, etc.):

_____

_____

Additional Notes:

Date: _____   Tank name/ID: _____

Data

Water level:	_____	Ammonia level:	_____
Temperature:	_____	Nitrite level:	_____
pH level:	_____	Nitrate level:	_____
Alkalinity:	_____	Salinity:	_____
Calcium level:	_____	Phosphate level:	_____
Iodine level:	_____	Magnesium level:	_____

Cleaning checklist

Water change? ☐ yes ☐ no   Amount changed: _____

☐ Glass   ☐ Gravel   ☐ Top   ☐ Other _____

Maintenance Checklist

notes

☐ Filters   ☐ rinse   ☐ replace   _____

☐ Pumps   _____

☐ Tubing   _____

☐ Connections   _____

☐ Airstones   _____

☐ Skimmers, etc.   _____

☐ Lighting   _____

Restock (food, treatments, equipment, etc.):

_____

_____

Additional Notes:

Date: _____ Tank name/ID: _____

Data

Water level:	_____	Ammonia level:	_____
Temperature:	_____	Nitrite level:	_____
pH level:	_____	Nitrate level:	_____
Alkalinity:	_____	Salinity:	_____
Calcium level:	_____	Phosphate level:	_____
Iodine level:	_____	Magnesium level:	_____

Cleaning checklist

Water change? ☐ yes ☐ no   Amount changed: _____

☐ Glass   ☐ Gravel   ☐ Top   ☐ Other _____

Maintenance Checklist

notes

☐ Filters   ☐ rinse   ☐ replace   _____

☐ Pumps   _____

☐ Tubing   _____

☐ Connections   _____

☐ Airstones   _____

☐ Skimmers, etc.   _____

☐ Lighting   _____

Restock (food, treatments, equipment, etc.):

_____

_____

Additional Notes:

Date: _____ Tank name/ID: _____

Data

Water level:	_____	Ammonia level:	_____
Temperature:	_____	Nitrite level:	_____
pH level:	_____	Nitrate level:	_____
Alkalinity:	_____	Salinity:	_____
Calcium level:	_____	Phosphate level:	_____
Iodine level:	_____	Magnesium level:	_____

Cleaning checklist

Water change? ☐ yes ☐ no   Amount changed: _____

☐ Glass   ☐ Gravel   ☐ Top   ☐ Other _____

Maintenance Checklist

notes

☐ Filters   ☐ rinse   ☐ replace   _____

☐ Pumps   _____

☐ Tubing   _____

☐ Connections   _____

☐ Airstones   _____

☐ Skimmers, etc.   _____

☐ Lighting   _____

Restock (food, treatments, equipment, etc.):

_____

_____

Additional Notes:

Date: _____ **Tank name/ID:** _____

Data

Water level:	_____	Ammonia level:	_____
Temperature:	_____	Nitrite level:	_____
pH level:	_____	Nitrate level:	_____
Alkalinity:	_____	Salinity:	_____
Calcium level:	_____	Phosphate level:	_____
Iodine level:	_____	Magnesium level:	_____

Cleaning checklist

Water change? ☐ yes ☐ no   Amount changed: _____

☐ Glass   ☐ Gravel   ☐ Top   ☐ Other _____

Maintenance Checklist

notes

☐ Filters   ☐ rinse   ☐ replace   _____

☐ Pumps   _____

☐ Tubing   _____

☐ Connections   _____

☐ Airstones   _____

☐ Skimmers, etc.   _____

☐ Lighting   _____

Restock (food, treatments, equipment, etc.):

_____

_____

Additional Notes:

Date: _____ Tank name/ID: _____

Data

Water level:	_____	Ammonia level:	_____
Temperature:	_____	Nitrite level:	_____
pH level:	_____	Nitrate level:	_____
Alkalinity:	_____	Salinity:	_____
Calcium level:	_____	Phosphate level:	_____
Iodine level:	_____	Magnesium level:	_____

Cleaning checklist

Water change? ☐ yes ☐ no   Amount changed: _____

☐ Glass   ☐ Gravel   ☐ Top   ☐ Other _____

Maintenance Checklist

notes

☐ Filters   ☐ rinse   ☐ replace   _____
☐ Pumps   _____
☐ Tubing   _____
☐ Connections   _____
☐ Airstones   _____
☐ Skimmers, etc.   _____
☐ Lighting   _____

Restock (food, treatments, equipment, etc.):
_____
_____

Additional Notes:

Date: _____ Tank name/ID: _____

Data

Water level:	_____	Ammonia level:	_____
Temperature:	_____	Nitrite level:	_____
pH level:	_____	Nitrate level:	_____
Alkalinity:	_____	Salinity:	_____
Calcium level:	_____	Phosphate level:	_____
Iodine level:	_____	Magnesium level:	_____

Cleaning checklist

Water change? ☐ yes ☐ no   Amount changed: _____

☐ Glass   ☐ Gravel   ☐ Top   ☐ Other _____

Maintenance Checklist

notes

☐ Filters   ☐ rinse   ☐ replace   _____

☐ Pumps   _____

☐ Tubing   _____

☐ Connections   _____

☐ Airstones   _____

☐ Skimmers, etc.   _____

☐ Lighting   _____

Restock (food, treatments, equipment, etc.):

_____

_____

Additional Notes:

Date: **Tank name/ID:**

Data

Water level: _____	Ammonia level:	_____
Temperature: _____	Nitrite level:	_____
pH level: _____	Nitrate level:	_____
Alkalinity: _____	Salinity:	_____
Calcium level: _____	Phosphate level:	_____
Iodine level: _____	Magnesium level:	_____

Cleaning checklist

Water change? ☐ yes ☐ no   Amount changed: _____

☐ Glass   ☐ Gravel   ☐ Top   ☐ Other _____

Maintenance Checklist

<u>notes</u>

☐ Filters   ☐ rinse   ☐ replace   _____

☐ Pumps   _____

☐ Tubing   _____

☐ Connections   _____

☐ Airstones   _____

☐ Skimmers, etc.   _____

☐ Lighting   _____

Restock (food, treatments, equipment, etc.):

_____

_____

Additional Notes:

Date: Tank name/ID:

Data

Water level: _____   Ammonia level: _____

Temperature: _____   Nitrite level: _____

pH level: _____   Nitrate level: _____

Alkalinity: _____   Salinity: _____

Calcium level: _____   Phosphate level: _____

Iodine level: _____   Magnesium level: _____

Cleaning checklist

Water change? ☐ yes ☐ no   Amount changed: _____

☐ Glass   ☐ Gravel   ☐ Top   ☐ Other _____

Maintenance Checklist

notes

☐ Filters   ☐ rinse   ☐ replace   _____

☐ Pumps   _____

☐ Tubing   _____

☐ Connections   _____

☐ Airstones   _____

☐ Skimmers, etc.   _____

☐ Lighting   _____

Restock (food, treatments, equipment, etc.):

_____

_____

Additional Notes:

Date: **Tank name/ID:**

Data

Water level:	_____	Ammonia level:	_____
Temperature:	_____	Nitrite level:	_____
pH level:	_____	Nitrate level:	_____
Alkalinity:	_____	Salinity:	_____
Calcium level:	_____	Phosphate level:	_____
Iodine level:	_____	Magnesium level:	_____

Cleaning checklist

Water change? ☐ yes ☐ no   Amount changed: _____

☐ Glass   ☐ Gravel   ☐ Top   ☐ Other _____

Maintenance Checklist

<u>notes</u>

☐ Filters   ☐ rinse   ☐ replace   _____

☐ Pumps   _____

☐ Tubing   _____

☐ Connections   _____

☐ Airstones   _____

☐ Skimmers, etc.   _____

☐ Lighting   _____

Restock (food, treatments, equipment, etc.):

_____

_____

Additional Notes:

Date: _____ Tank name/ID: _____

Data

Water level:	_____	Ammonia level:	_____
Temperature:	_____	Nitrite level:	_____
pH level:	_____	Nitrate level:	_____
Alkalinity:	_____	Salinity:	_____
Calcium level:	_____	Phosphate level:	_____
Iodine level:	_____	Magnesium level:	_____

Cleaning checklist

Water change? ☐ yes ☐ no   Amount changed: _____

☐ Glass   ☐ Gravel   ☐ Top   ☐ Other _____

Maintenance Checklist

notes

☐ Filters ☐ rinse ☐ replace _____

☐ Pumps _____

☐ Tubing _____

☐ Connections _____

☐ Airstones _____

☐ Skimmers, etc. _____

☐ Lighting _____

Restock (food, treatments, equipment, etc.):

_____

_____

Additional Notes:

Date: **Tank name/ID:**

Data

Water level:	_____	Ammonia level:	_____
Temperature:	_____	Nitrite level:	_____
pH level:	_____	Nitrate level:	_____
Alkalinity:	_____	Salinity:	_____
Calcium level:	_____	Phosphate level:	_____
Iodine level:	_____	Magnesium level:	_____

Cleaning checklist

Water change? ☐ yes ☐ no   Amount changed: _____

☐ Glass   ☐ Gravel   ☐ Top   ☐ Other _____

Maintenance Checklist

<u>notes</u>

☐ Filters   ☐ rinse   ☐ replace   _____

☐ Pumps   _____

☐ Tubing   _____

☐ Connections   _____

☐ Airstones   _____

☐ Skimmers, etc.   _____

☐ Lighting   _____

Restock (food, treatments, equipment, etc.):

_____

_____

Additional Notes:

Date: **Tank name/ID:**

Data

Water level:	_____	Ammonia level:	_____
Temperature:	_____	Nitrite level:	_____
pH level:	_____	Nitrate level:	_____
Alkalinity:	_____	Salinity:	_____
Calcium level:	_____	Phosphate level:	_____
Iodine level:	_____	Magnesium level:	_____

Cleaning checklist

Water change? ☐ yes ☐ no   Amount changed: _____

☐ Glass ☐ Gravel ☐ Top ☐ Other _____

Maintenance Checklist

notes

☐ Filters ☐ rinse ☐ replace _____

☐ Pumps _____

☐ Tubing _____

☐ Connections _____

☐ Airstones _____

☐ Skimmers, etc. _____

☐ Lighting _____

Restock (food, treatments, equipment, etc.):

_____

_____

Additional Notes:

Date: **Tank name/ID:**

Data

Water level:	_____	Ammonia level:	_____
Temperature:	_____	Nitrite level:	_____
pH level:	_____	Nitrate level:	_____
Alkalinity:	_____	Salinity:	_____
Calcium level:	_____	Phosphate level:	_____
Iodine level:	_____	Magnesium level:	_____

Cleaning checklist

Water change? ☐ yes ☐ no   Amount changed: _____

☐ Glass   ☐ Gravel   ☐ Top   ☐ Other _____

Maintenance Checklist

<u>notes</u>

☐ Filters   ☐ rinse   ☐ replace   _____

☐ Pumps   _____

☐ Tubing   _____

☐ Connections   _____

☐ Airstones   _____

☐ Skimmers, etc.   _____

☐ Lighting   _____

Restock (food, treatments, equipment, etc.):

_____

_____

Additional Notes:

Date: _____ Tank name/ID: _____

Data

Water level:	_____	Ammonia level:	_____
Temperature:	_____	Nitrite level:	_____
pH level:	_____	Nitrate level:	_____
Alkalinity:	_____	Salinity:	_____
Calcium level:	_____	Phosphate level:	_____
Iodine level:	_____	Magnesium level:	_____

Cleaning checklist

Water change? ☐ yes ☐ no   Amount changed: _____

☐ Glass   ☐ Gravel   ☐ Top   ☐ Other _____

Maintenance Checklist

notes

☐ Filters   ☐ rinse   ☐ replace   _____

☐ Pumps   _____

☐ Tubing   _____

☐ Connections   _____

☐ Airstones   _____

☐ Skimmers, etc.   _____

☐ Lighting   _____

Restock (food, treatments, equipment, etc.):

_____

_____

Additional Notes:

Date: Tank name/ID:

Data

Water level:	_____	Ammonia level:	_____
Temperature:	_____	Nitrite level:	_____
pH level:	_____	Nitrate level:	_____
Alkalinity:	_____	Salinity:	_____
Calcium level:	_____	Phosphate level:	_____
Iodine level:	_____	Magnesium level:	_____

Cleaning checklist

Water change? ☐ yes ☐ no   Amount changed: _____

☐ Glass   ☐ Gravel   ☐ Top   ☐ Other _____

Maintenance Checklist

notes

☐ Filters   ☐ rinse   ☐ replace   _____

☐ Pumps   _____

☐ Tubing   _____

☐ Connections   _____

☐ Airstones   _____

☐ Skimmers, etc.   _____

☐ Lighting   _____

Restock (food, treatments, equipment, etc.):

_____

_____

Additional Notes:

Date: **Tank name/ID:**

Data

Water level:	_____	Ammonia level:	_____
Temperature:	_____	Nitrite level:	_____
pH level:	_____	Nitrate level:	_____
Alkalinity:	_____	Salinity:	_____
Calcium level:	_____	Phosphate level:	_____
Iodine level:	_____	Magnesium level:	_____

Cleaning checklist

Water change? ☐ yes ☐ no   Amount changed: _____

☐ Glass   ☐ Gravel   ☐ Top   ☐ Other _____

Maintenance Checklist

<u>notes</u>

☐ Filters   ☐ rinse   ☐ replace   _____

☐ Pumps   _____

☐ Tubing   _____

☐ Connections   _____

☐ Airstones   _____

☐ Skimmers, etc.   _____

☐ Lighting   _____

Restock (food, treatments, equipment, etc.):

_____

_____

Additional Notes:

Date: _____ **Tank name/ID:** _____

Data

Water level:	_____	Ammonia level:	_____
Temperature:	_____	Nitrite level:	_____
pH level:	_____	Nitrate level:	_____
Alkalinity:	_____	Salinity:	_____
Calcium level:	_____	Phosphate level:	_____
Iodine level:	_____	Magnesium level:	_____

Cleaning checklist

Water change? ☐ yes ☐ no   Amount changed: _____

☐ Glass   ☐ Gravel   ☐ Top   ☐ Other _____

Maintenance Checklist

notes

☐ Filters   ☐ rinse   ☐ replace   _____

☐ Pumps   _____

☐ Tubing   _____

☐ Connections   _____

☐ Airstones   _____

☐ Skimmers, etc.   _____

☐ Lighting   _____

Restock (food, treatments, equipment, etc.):

_____

_____

Additional Notes:

Date: Tank name/ID:

Data

Water level:	_____	Ammonia level:	_____
Temperature:	_____	Nitrite level:	_____
pH level:	_____	Nitrate level:	_____
Alkalinity:	_____	Salinity:	_____
Calcium level:	_____	Phosphate level:	_____
Iodine level:	_____	Magnesium level:	_____

Cleaning checklist

Water change? ☐ yes ☐ no   Amount changed: _____

☐ Glass   ☐ Gravel   ☐ Top   ☐ Other _____

Maintenance Checklist

notes

☐ Filters   ☐ rinse   ☐ replace   _____

☐ Pumps   _____

☐ Tubing   _____

☐ Connections   _____

☐ Airstones   _____

☐ Skimmers, etc.   _____

☐ Lighting   _____

Restock (food, treatments, equipment, etc.):

_____

_____

Additional Notes:

Date: _____   Tank name/ID: _____

Data

Water level:	_____	Ammonia level:	_____
Temperature:	_____	Nitrite level:	_____
pH level:	_____	Nitrate level:	_____
Alkalinity:	_____	Salinity:	_____
Calcium level:	_____	Phosphate level:	_____
Iodine level:	_____	Magnesium level:	_____

Cleaning checklist

Water change? ☐ yes ☐ no   Amount changed: _____

☐ Glass   ☐ Gravel   ☐ Top   ☐ Other _____

Maintenance Checklist

notes

☐ Filters   ☐ rinse   ☐ replace   _____

☐ Pumps   _____

☐ Tubing   _____

☐ Connections   _____

☐ Airstones   _____

☐ Skimmers, etc.   _____

☐ Lighting   _____

Restock (food, treatments, equipment, etc.):

_____

_____

Additional Notes:

Date: _____   Tank name/ID: _____

Data

Water level:	_____	Ammonia level:	_____
Temperature:	_____	Nitrite level:	_____
pH level:	_____	Nitrate level:	_____
Alkalinity:	_____	Salinity:	_____
Calcium level:	_____	Phosphate level:	_____
Iodine level:	_____	Magnesium level:	_____

Cleaning checklist

Water change? ☐ yes ☐ no   Amount changed: _____

☐ Glass   ☐ Gravel   ☐ Top   ☐ Other _____

Maintenance Checklist

notes

☐ Filters   ☐ rinse   ☐ replace   _____

☐ Pumps   _____

☐ Tubing   _____

☐ Connections   _____

☐ Airstones   _____

☐ Skimmers, etc.   _____

☐ Lighting   _____

Restock (food, treatments, equipment, etc.):

_____

_____

Additional Notes:

Date: Tank name/ID:

Data

Water level:	_____	Ammonia level:	_____
Temperature:	_____	Nitrite level:	_____
pH level:	_____	Nitrate level:	_____
Alkalinity:	_____	Salinity:	_____
Calcium level:	_____	Phosphate level:	_____
Iodine level:	_____	Magnesium level:	_____

Cleaning checklist

Water change? ☐ yes ☐ no   Amount changed: _____

☐ Glass   ☐ Gravel   ☐ Top   ☐ Other _____

Maintenance Checklist

notes

☐ Filters   ☐ rinse   ☐ replace   _____
☐ Pumps   _____
☐ Tubing   _____
☐ Connections _____
☐ Airstones _____
☐ Skimmers, etc. _____
☐ Lighting _____

Restock (food, treatments, equipment, etc.):

_____
_____

Additional Notes:

Date: _____ Tank name/ID: _____

Data

Water level:	_____	Ammonia level:	_____
Temperature:	_____	Nitrite level:	_____
pH level:	_____	Nitrate level:	_____
Alkalinity:	_____	Salinity:	_____
Calcium level:	_____	Phosphate level:	_____
Iodine level:	_____	Magnesium level:	_____

Cleaning checklist

Water change? ☐ yes ☐ no   Amount changed: _____

☐ Glass   ☐ Gravel   ☐ Top   ☐ Other _____

Maintenance Checklist

notes

☐ Filters   ☐ rinse   ☐ replace   _____

☐ Pumps   _____

☐ Tubing   _____

☐ Connections   _____

☐ Airstones   _____

☐ Skimmers, etc.   _____

☐ Lighting   _____

Restock (food, treatments, equipment, etc.):

_____

_____

Additional Notes:

Date: _____ Tank name/ID: _____

Data

Water level:	_____	Ammonia level:	_____
Temperature:	_____	Nitrite level:	_____
pH level:	_____	Nitrate level:	_____
Alkalinity:	_____	Salinity:	_____
Calcium level:	_____	Phosphate level:	_____
Iodine level:	_____	Magnesium level:	_____

Cleaning checklist

Water change? ☐ yes ☐ no   Amount changed: _____

☐ Glass   ☐ Gravel   ☐ Top   ☐ Other _____

Maintenance Checklist

notes

☐ Filters   ☐ rinse   ☐ replace   _____

☐ Pumps   _____

☐ Tubing   _____

☐ Connections   _____

☐ Airstones   _____

☐ Skimmers, etc.   _____

☐ Lighting   _____

Restock (food, treatments, equipment, etc.):
_____
_____

Additional Notes:

Date: Tank name/ID:

Data

Water level:	_____	Ammonia level:	_____
Temperature:	_____	Nitrite level:	_____
pH level:	_____	Nitrate level:	_____
Alkalinity:	_____	Salinity:	_____
Calcium level:	_____	Phosphate level:	_____
Iodine level:	_____	Magnesium level:	_____

Cleaning checklist

Water change? ☐ yes ☐ no   Amount changed: _____

☐ Glass   ☐ Gravel   ☐ Top   ☐ Other _____

Maintenance Checklist

notes

☐ Filters   ☐ rinse   ☐ replace   _____

☐ Pumps   _____

☐ Tubing   _____

☐ Connections   _____

☐ Airstones   _____

☐ Skimmers, etc.   _____

☐ Lighting   _____

Restock (food, treatments, equipment, etc.):

_____

_____

Additional Notes:

Date: Tank name/ID:

Data

Water level:	_____	Ammonia level:	_____
Temperature:	_____	Nitrite level:	_____
pH level:	_____	Nitrate level:	_____
Alkalinity:	_____	Salinity:	_____
Calcium level:	_____	Phosphate level:	_____
Iodine level:	_____	Magnesium level:	_____

Cleaning checklist

Water change? ☐ yes ☐ no   Amount changed: _____

☐ Glass   ☐ Gravel   ☐ Top   ☐ Other _____

Maintenance Checklist

notes

☐ Filters   ☐ rinse ☐ replace _____

☐ Pumps _____

☐ Tubing _____

☐ Connections _____

☐ Airstones _____

☐ Skimmers, etc. _____

☐ Lighting _____

Restock (food, treatments, equipment, etc.):

_____

_____

Additional Notes:

Date: _____ Tank name/ID: _____

Data

Water level:	_____	Ammonia level:	_____
Temperature:	_____	Nitrite level:	_____
pH level:	_____	Nitrate level:	_____
Alkalinity:	_____	Salinity:	_____
Calcium level:	_____	Phosphate level:	_____
Iodine level:	_____	Magnesium level:	_____

Cleaning checklist

Water change? ☐ yes ☐ no   Amount changed: _____

☐ Glass   ☐ Gravel   ☐ Top   ☐ Other _____

Maintenance Checklist

notes

☐ Filters   ☐ rinse   ☐ replace   _____

☐ Pumps   _____

☐ Tubing   _____

☐ Connections   _____

☐ Airstones   _____

☐ Skimmers, etc.   _____

☐ Lighting   _____

Restock (food, treatments, equipment, etc.):

_____

_____

Additional Notes:

Date: _____   Tank name/ID: _____

Data

Water level: _____   Ammonia level: _____

Temperature: _____   Nitrite level: _____

pH level: _____   Nitrate level: _____

Alkalinity: _____   Salinity: _____

Calcium level: _____   Phosphate level: _____

Iodine level: _____   Magnesium level: _____

Cleaning checklist

Water change? ☐ yes ☐ no   Amount changed: _____

☐ Glass   ☐ Gravel   ☐ Top   ☐ Other _____

Maintenance Checklist

notes

☐ Filters   ☐ rinse   ☐ replace   _____

☐ Pumps   _____

☐ Tubing   _____

☐ Connections   _____

☐ Airstones   _____

☐ Skimmers, etc.   _____

☐ Lighting   _____

Restock (food, treatments, equipment, etc.):

_____

_____

Additional Notes:

Date: Tank name/ID:

Data

Water level:	_____	Ammonia level:	_____
Temperature:	_____	Nitrite level:	_____
pH level:	_____	Nitrate level:	_____
Alkalinity:	_____	Salinity:	_____
Calcium level:	_____	Phosphate level:	_____
Iodine level:	_____	Magnesium level:	_____

Cleaning checklist

Water change? ☐ yes ☐ no   Amount changed: _____

☐ Glass   ☐ Gravel   ☐ Top   ☐ Other _____

Maintenance Checklist

notes

☐ Filters   ☐ rinse   ☐ replace   _____

☐ Pumps   _____

☐ Tubing   _____

☐ Connections   _____

☐ Airstones   _____

☐ Skimmers, etc.   _____

☐ Lighting   _____

Restock (food, treatments, equipment, etc.):

_____

_____

Additional Notes:

Date: _____ Tank name/ID: _____

Data

Water level: _____ Ammonia level: _____

Temperature: _____ Nitrite level: _____

pH level: _____ Nitrate level: _____

Alkalinity: _____ Salinity: _____

Calcium level: _____ Phosphate level: _____

Iodine level: _____ Magnesium level: _____

Cleaning checklist

Water change? ☐ yes ☐ no   Amount changed: _____

☐ Glass   ☐ Gravel   ☐ Top   ☐ Other _____

Maintenance Checklist

notes

☐ Filters   ☐ rinse   ☐ replace   _____

☐ Pumps   _____

☐ Tubing   _____

☐ Connections   _____

☐ Airstones   _____

☐ Skimmers, etc.   _____

☐ Lighting   _____

Restock (food, treatments, equipment, etc.):

_____

_____

Additional Notes:

Date: Tank name/ID:

Data

Water level:	_____	Ammonia level:	_____
Temperature:	_____	Nitrite level:	_____
pH level:	_____	Nitrate level:	_____
Alkalinity:	_____	Salinity:	_____
Calcium level:	_____	Phosphate level:	_____
Iodine level:	_____	Magnesium level:	_____

Cleaning checklist

Water change? ☐ yes ☐ no   Amount changed: _____

☐ Glass   ☐ Gravel   ☐ Top   ☐ Other _____

Maintenance Checklist

<u>notes</u>

☐ Filters   ☐ rinse   ☐ replace   _____

☐ Pumps   _____

☐ Tubing   _____

☐ Connections   _____

☐ Airstones   _____

☐ Skimmers, etc.   _____

☐ Lighting   _____

Restock (food, treatments, equipment, etc.):

_____

_____

Additional Notes:

Date: Tank name/ID:

Data

Water level:	_____	Ammonia level:	_____
Temperature:	_____	Nitrite level:	_____
pH level:	_____	Nitrate level:	_____
Alkalinity:	_____	Salinity:	_____
Calcium level:	_____	Phosphate level:	_____
Iodine level:	_____	Magnesium level:	_____

Cleaning checklist

Water change? ☐ yes ☐ no   Amount changed: _____

☐ Glass   ☐ Gravel   ☐ Top   ☐ Other _____

Maintenance Checklist

notes

☐ Filters   ☐ rinse   ☐ replace   _____

☐ Pumps   _____

☐ Tubing   _____

☐ Connections   _____

☐ Airstones   _____

☐ Skimmers, etc.   _____

☐ Lighting   _____

Restock (food, treatments, equipment, etc.):

_____

_____

Additional Notes:

Date: _____ Tank name/ID: _____

Data

Water level:	_____	Ammonia level:	_____
Temperature:	_____	Nitrite level:	_____
pH level:	_____	Nitrate level:	_____
Alkalinity:	_____	Salinity:	_____
Calcium level:	_____	Phosphate level:	_____
Iodine level:	_____	Magnesium level:	_____

Cleaning checklist

Water change? ☐ yes ☐ no   Amount changed: _____

☐ Glass   ☐ Gravel   ☐ Top   ☐ Other _____

Maintenance Checklist

notes

☐ Filters   ☐ rinse   ☐ replace   _____

☐ Pumps   _____

☐ Tubing   _____

☐ Connections   _____

☐ Airstones   _____

☐ Skimmers, etc.   _____

☐ Lighting   _____

Restock (food, treatments, equipment, etc.):

_____

_____

Additional Notes:

Date: _____   Tank name/ID: _____

Data

Water level:	_____	Ammonia level:	_____
Temperature:	_____	Nitrite level:	_____
pH level:	_____	Nitrate level:	_____
Alkalinity:	_____	Salinity:	_____
Calcium level:	_____	Phosphate level:	_____
Iodine level:	_____	Magnesium level:	_____

Cleaning checklist

Water change? ☐ yes ☐ no   Amount changed: _____

☐ Glass   ☐ Gravel   ☐ Top   ☐ Other _____

Maintenance Checklist

notes

☐ Filters   ☐ rinse   ☐ replace   _____

☐ Pumps   _____

☐ Tubing   _____

☐ Connections   _____

☐ Airstones   _____

☐ Skimmers, etc.   _____

☐ Lighting   _____

Restock (food, treatments, equipment, etc.):

_____

_____

Additional Notes:

Date: _____ Tank name/ID: _____

Data

Water level:	_____	Ammonia level:	_____
Temperature:	_____	Nitrite level:	_____
pH level:	_____	Nitrate level:	_____
Alkalinity:	_____	Salinity:	_____
Calcium level:	_____	Phosphate level:	_____
Iodine level:	_____	Magnesium level:	_____

Cleaning checklist

Water change? ☐ yes ☐ no   Amount changed: _____

☐ Glass   ☐ Gravel   ☐ Top   ☐ Other _____

Maintenance Checklist

notes

☐ Filters   ☐ rinse   ☐ replace   _____

☐ Pumps   _____

☐ Tubing   _____

☐ Connections   _____

☐ Airstones   _____

☐ Skimmers, etc.   _____

☐ Lighting   _____

Restock (food, treatments, equipment, etc.):

_____

_____

Additional Notes:

Date: _____   Tank name/ID: _____

Data

Water level:	_____	Ammonia level:	_____
Temperature:	_____	Nitrite level:	_____
pH level:	_____	Nitrate level:	_____
Alkalinity:	_____	Salinity:	_____
Calcium level:	_____	Phosphate level:	_____
Iodine level:	_____	Magnesium level:	_____

Cleaning checklist

Water change? ☐ yes ☐ no   Amount changed: _____

☐ Glass   ☐ Gravel   ☐ Top   ☐ Other _____

Maintenance Checklist

notes

☐ Filters   ☐ rinse   ☐ replace   _____

☐ Pumps   _____

☐ Tubing   _____

☐ Connections   _____

☐ Airstones   _____

☐ Skimmers, etc.   _____

☐ Lighting   _____

Restock (food, treatments, equipment, etc.):

_____

_____

Additional Notes:

Date: _____   Tank name/ID: _____

Data

Water level:	_____	Ammonia level:	_____
Temperature:	_____	Nitrite level:	_____
pH level:	_____	Nitrate level:	_____
Alkalinity:	_____	Salinity:	_____
Calcium level:	_____	Phosphate level:	_____
Iodine level:	_____	Magnesium level:	_____

Cleaning checklist

Water change? ☐ yes ☐ no   Amount changed: _____

☐ Glass   ☐ Gravel   ☐ Top   ☐ Other _____

Maintenance Checklist

notes

☐ Filters   ☐ rinse   ☐ replace   _____
☐ Pumps   _____
☐ Tubing   _____
☐ Connections   _____
☐ Airstones   _____
☐ Skimmers, etc.   _____
☐ Lighting   _____

Restock (food, treatments, equipment, etc.):

_____

_____

Additional Notes:

Date: _____ Tank name/ID: _____

Data

Water level:	_____	Ammonia level:	_____
Temperature:	_____	Nitrite level:	_____
pH level:	_____	Nitrate level:	_____
Alkalinity:	_____	Salinity:	_____
Calcium level:	_____	Phosphate level:	_____
Iodine level:	_____	Magnesium level:	_____

Cleaning checklist

Water change? ☐ yes ☐ no   Amount changed: _____

☐ Glass   ☐ Gravel   ☐ Top   ☐ Other _____

Maintenance Checklist

notes

☐ Filters   ☐ rinse ☐ replace   _____

☐ Pumps   _____

☐ Tubing   _____

☐ Connections   _____

☐ Airstones   _____

☐ Skimmers, etc.   _____

☐ Lighting   _____

Restock (food, treatments, equipment, etc.):

_____

_____

Additional Notes:

Date: _____ Tank name/ID: _____

Data

Water level:	_____	Ammonia level:	_____
Temperature:	_____	Nitrite level:	_____
pH level:	_____	Nitrate level:	_____
Alkalinity:	_____	Salinity:	_____
Calcium level:	_____	Phosphate level:	_____
Iodine level:	_____	Magnesium level:	_____

Cleaning checklist

Water change? ☐ yes ☐ no   Amount changed: _____

☐ Glass   ☐ Gravel   ☐ Top   ☐ Other _____

Maintenance Checklist

notes

☐ Filters   ☐ rinse   ☐ replace   _____

☐ Pumps   _____

☐ Tubing   _____

☐ Connections   _____

☐ Airstones   _____

☐ Skimmers, etc.   _____

☐ Lighting   _____

Restock (food, treatments, equipment, etc.):

_____

_____

Additional Notes:

Date: _____ Tank name/ID: _____

Data

Water level:	_____	Ammonia level:	_____
Temperature:	_____	Nitrite level:	_____
pH level:	_____	Nitrate level:	_____
Alkalinity:	_____	Salinity:	_____
Calcium level:	_____	Phosphate level:	_____
Iodine level:	_____	Magnesium level:	_____

Cleaning checklist

Water change? ☐ yes ☐ no   Amount changed: _____

☐ Glass   ☐ Gravel   ☐ Top   ☐ Other _____

Maintenance Checklist

notes

☐ Filters ☐ rinse ☐ replace _____

☐ Pumps _____

☐ Tubing _____

☐ Connections _____

☐ Airstones _____

☐ Skimmers, etc. _____

☐ Lighting _____

Restock (food, treatments, equipment, etc.):

_____

_____

Additional Notes:

Date: Tank name/ID:

Data

Water level:	_____	Ammonia level:	_____
Temperature:	_____	Nitrite level:	_____
pH level:	_____	Nitrate level:	_____
Alkalinity:	_____	Salinity:	_____
Calcium level:	_____	Phosphate level:	_____
Iodine level:	_____	Magnesium level:	_____

Cleaning checklist

Water change? ☐ yes ☐ no   Amount changed: _____

☐ Glass   ☐ Gravel   ☐ Top   ☐ Other _____

Maintenance Checklist

notes

☐ Filters   ☐ rinse   ☐ replace   _____

☐ Pumps   _____

☐ Tubing   _____

☐ Connections   _____

☐ Airstones   _____

☐ Skimmers, etc.   _____

☐ Lighting   _____

Restock (food, treatments, equipment, etc.):

_____

_____

Additional Notes:

Date: _____ Tank name/ID: _____

Data

Water level:	_____	Ammonia level:	_____
Temperature:	_____	Nitrite level:	_____
pH level:	_____	Nitrate level:	_____
Alkalinity:	_____	Salinity:	_____
Calcium level:	_____	Phosphate level:	_____
Iodine level:	_____	Magnesium level:	_____

Cleaning checklist

Water change? ☐ yes ☐ no Amount changed: _____

☐ Glass ☐ Gravel ☐ Top ☐ Other _____

Maintenance Checklist

notes

☐ Filters ☐ rinse ☐ replace _____
☐ Pumps _____
☐ Tubing _____
☐ Connections _____
☐ Airstones _____
☐ Skimmers, etc. _____
☐ Lighting _____

Restock (food, treatments, equipment, etc.):
_____
_____

Additional Notes:

Date: _____   Tank name/ID: _____

Data

Water level:	_____	Ammonia level:	_____
Temperature:	_____	Nitrite level:	_____
pH level:	_____	Nitrate level:	_____
Alkalinity:	_____	Salinity:	_____
Calcium level:	_____	Phosphate level:	_____
Iodine level:	_____	Magnesium level:	_____

Cleaning checklist

Water change? ☐ yes ☐ no   Amount changed: _____

☐ Glass   ☐ Gravel   ☐ Top   ☐ Other _____

Maintenance Checklist

notes

☐ Filters   ☐ rinse   ☐ replace   _____

☐ Pumps   _____

☐ Tubing   _____

☐ Connections   _____

☐ Airstones   _____

☐ Skimmers, etc.   _____

☐ Lighting   _____

Restock (food, treatments, equipment, etc.):

_____

_____

Additional Notes:

Date: Tank name/ID:

Data

Water level:	_____	Ammonia level:	_____
Temperature:	_____	Nitrite level:	_____
pH level:	_____	Nitrate level:	_____
Alkalinity:	_____	Salinity:	_____
Calcium level:	_____	Phosphate level:	_____
Iodine level:	_____	Magnesium level:	_____

Cleaning checklist

Water change? ☐ yes ☐ no   Amount changed: _____

☐ Glass   ☐ Gravel   ☐ Top   ☐ Other _____

Maintenance Checklist

notes

☐ Filters   ☐ rinse   ☐ replace   _____

☐ Pumps   _____

☐ Tubing   _____

☐ Connections   _____

☐ Airstones   _____

☐ Skimmers, etc.   _____

☐ Lighting   _____

Restock (food, treatments, equipment, etc.):

_____

_____

Additional Notes:

Date: Tank name/ID:

Data

Water level:	_____	Ammonia level:	_____
Temperature:	_____	Nitrite level:	_____
pH level:	_____	Nitrate level:	_____
Alkalinity:	_____	Salinity:	_____
Calcium level:	_____	Phosphate level:	_____
Iodine level:	_____	Magnesium level:	_____

Cleaning checklist

Water change? ☐ yes ☐ no   Amount changed: _____

☐ Glass   ☐ Gravel   ☐ Top   ☐ Other _____

Maintenance Checklist

notes

☐ Filters   ☐ rinse   ☐ replace   _____

☐ Pumps   _____

☐ Tubing   _____

☐ Connections   _____

☐ Airstones   _____

☐ Skimmers, etc.   _____

☐ Lighting   _____

Restock (food, treatments, equipment, etc.):

_____

_____

Additional Notes:

Date: Tank name/ID:

Data

Water level:	_____	Ammonia level:	_____
Temperature:	_____	Nitrite level:	_____
pH level:	_____	Nitrate level:	_____
Alkalinity:	_____	Salinity:	_____
Calcium level:	_____	Phosphate level:	_____
Iodine level:	_____	Magnesium level:	_____

Cleaning checklist

Water change? ☐ yes ☐ no   Amount changed: _____

☐ Glass   ☐ Gravel   ☐ Top   ☐ Other _____

Maintenance Checklist

notes

☐ Filters   ☐ rinse   ☐ replace   _____

☐ Pumps   _____

☐ Tubing   _____

☐ Connections   _____

☐ Airstones   _____

☐ Skimmers, etc.   _____

☐ Lighting   _____

Restock (food, treatments, equipment, etc.):

_____

_____

Additional Notes:

Date: _____   Tank name/ID: _____

Data

Water level:	_____	Ammonia level:	_____
Temperature:	_____	Nitrite level:	_____
pH level:	_____	Nitrate level:	_____
Alkalinity:	_____	Salinity:	_____
Calcium level:	_____	Phosphate level:	_____
Iodine level:	_____	Magnesium level:	_____

Cleaning checklist

Water change? ☐ yes ☐ no   Amount changed: _____

☐ Glass   ☐ Gravel   ☐ Top   ☐ Other _____

Maintenance Checklist

notes

☐ Filters ☐ rinse ☐ replace   _____

☐ Pumps   _____

☐ Tubing   _____

☐ Connections   _____

☐ Airstones   _____

☐ Skimmers, etc.   _____

☐ Lighting   _____

Restock (food, treatments, equipment, etc.):

_____

_____

Additional Notes:

Date: Tank name/ID:

Data

Water level:	_____	Ammonia level:	_____
Temperature:	_____	Nitrite level:	_____
pH level:	_____	Nitrate level:	_____
Alkalinity:	_____	Salinity:	_____
Calcium level:	_____	Phosphate level:	_____
Iodine level:	_____	Magnesium level:	_____

Cleaning checklist

Water change? ☐ yes ☐ no   Amount changed: _____

☐ Glass ☐ Gravel ☐ Top ☐ Other _____

Maintenance Checklist

<u>notes</u>

☐ Filters ☐ rinse ☐ replace _____

☐ Pumps _____

☐ Tubing _____

☐ Connections _____

☐ Airstones _____

☐ Skimmers, etc. _____

☐ Lighting _____

Restock (food, treatments, equipment, etc.):

_____

_____

Additional Notes:

Date: _____ Tank name/ID: _____

Data

Water level:	_____	Ammonia level:	_____
Temperature:	_____	Nitrite level:	_____
pH level:	_____	Nitrate level:	_____
Alkalinity:	_____	Salinity:	_____
Calcium level:	_____	Phosphate level:	_____
Iodine level:	_____	Magnesium level:	_____

Cleaning checklist

Water change? ☐ yes ☐ no   Amount changed: _____

☐ Glass   ☐ Gravel   ☐ Top   ☐ Other _____

Maintenance Checklist

notes

☐ Filters   ☐ rinse   ☐ replace   _____

☐ Pumps   _____

☐ Tubing   _____

☐ Connections   _____

☐ Airstones   _____

☐ Skimmers, etc.   _____

☐ Lighting   _____

Restock (food, treatments, equipment, etc.):

_____

_____

Additional Notes:

Date: _____ Tank name/ID: _____

Data

Water level:	_____	Ammonia level:	_____
Temperature:	_____	Nitrite level:	_____
pH level:	_____	Nitrate level:	_____
Alkalinity:	_____	Salinity:	_____
Calcium level:	_____	Phosphate level:	_____
Iodine level:	_____	Magnesium level:	_____

Cleaning checklist

Water change? ☐ yes ☐ no   Amount changed: _____

☐ Glass   ☐ Gravel   ☐ Top   ☐ Other _____

Maintenance Checklist

notes

☐ Filters   ☐ rinse   ☐ replace   _____

☐ Pumps   _____

☐ Tubing   _____

☐ Connections   _____

☐ Airstones   _____

☐ Skimmers, etc.   _____

☐ Lighting   _____

Restock (food, treatments, equipment, etc.):

_____

_____

Additional Notes:

Date: _____   Tank name/ID: _____

Data

Water level:	_____	Ammonia level:	_____
Temperature:	_____	Nitrite level:	_____
pH level:	_____	Nitrate level:	_____
Alkalinity:	_____	Salinity:	_____
Calcium level:	_____	Phosphate level:	_____
Iodine level:	_____	Magnesium level:	_____

Cleaning checklist

Water change? ☐ yes ☐ no   Amount changed: _____

☐ Glass   ☐ Gravel   ☐ Top   ☐ Other _____

Maintenance Checklist

notes

☐ Filters   ☐ rinse   ☐ replace   _____

☐ Pumps   _____

☐ Tubing   _____

☐ Connections   _____

☐ Airstones   _____

☐ Skimmers, etc.   _____

☐ Lighting   _____

Restock (food, treatments, equipment, etc.):

_____

_____

Additional Notes:

Date: _____ Tank name/ID: _____

Data

Water level: _____   Ammonia level: _____

Temperature: _____   Nitrite level: _____

pH level: _____   Nitrate level: _____

Alkalinity: _____   Salinity: _____

Calcium level: _____   Phosphate level: _____

Iodine level: _____   Magnesium level: _____

Cleaning checklist

Water change? ☐ yes ☐ no   Amount changed: _____

☐ Glass   ☐ Gravel   ☐ Top   ☐ Other _____

Maintenance Checklist

notes

☐ Filters   ☐ rinse   ☐ replace   _____

☐ Pumps   _____

☐ Tubing   _____

☐ Connections   _____

☐ Airstones   _____

☐ Skimmers, etc.   _____

☐ Lighting   _____

Restock (food, treatments, equipment, etc.):

_____

_____

Additional Notes:

Date: _____ Tank name/ID: _____

Data

Water level:	_____	Ammonia level:	_____
Temperature:	_____	Nitrite level:	_____
pH level:	_____	Nitrate level:	_____
Alkalinity:	_____	Salinity:	_____
Calcium level:	_____	Phosphate level:	_____
Iodine level:	_____	Magnesium level:	_____

Cleaning checklist

Water change? ☐ yes ☐ no   Amount changed: _____

☐ Glass   ☐ Gravel   ☐ Top   ☐ Other _____

Maintenance Checklist

notes

☐ Filters   ☐ rinse   ☐ replace   _____

☐ Pumps   _____

☐ Tubing   _____

☐ Connections   _____

☐ Airstones   _____

☐ Skimmers, etc.   _____

☐ Lighting   _____

Restock (food, treatments, equipment, etc.):

_____

_____

Additional Notes:

Date: _____ Tank name/ID: _____

Data

Water level:	_____	Ammonia level:	_____
Temperature:	_____	Nitrite level:	_____
pH level:	_____	Nitrate level:	_____
Alkalinity:	_____	Salinity:	_____
Calcium level:	_____	Phosphate level:	_____
Iodine level:	_____	Magnesium level:	_____

Cleaning checklist

Water change? ☐ yes ☐ no   Amount changed: _____

☐ Glass   ☐ Gravel   ☐ Top   ☐ Other _____

Maintenance Checklist

notes

☐ Filters   ☐ rinse   ☐ replace   _____

☐ Pumps   _____

☐ Tubing   _____

☐ Connections   _____

☐ Airstones   _____

☐ Skimmers, etc.   _____

☐ Lighting   _____

Restock (food, treatments, equipment, etc.):

_____

_____

Additional Notes:

Date: _____   Tank name/ID: _____

Data

Water level:	_____	Ammonia level:	_____
Temperature:	_____	Nitrite level:	_____
pH level:	_____	Nitrate level:	_____
Alkalinity:	_____	Salinity:	_____
Calcium level:	_____	Phosphate level:	_____
Iodine level:	_____	Magnesium level:	_____

Cleaning checklist

Water change? ☐ yes ☐ no   Amount changed: _____

☐ Glass   ☐ Gravel   ☐ Top   ☐ Other _____

Maintenance Checklist

notes

☐ Filters   ☐ rinse   ☐ replace   _____
☐ Pumps   _____
☐ Tubing   _____
☐ Connections   _____
☐ Airstones   _____
☐ Skimmers, etc.   _____
☐ Lighting   _____

Restock (food, treatments, equipment, etc.):
_____
_____

Additional Notes:

Date: _____   Tank name/ID: _____

Data

Water level:	_____	Ammonia level:	_____
Temperature:	_____	Nitrite level:	_____
pH level:	_____	Nitrate level:	_____
Alkalinity:	_____	Salinity:	_____
Calcium level:	_____	Phosphate level:	_____
Iodine level:	_____	Magnesium level:	_____

Cleaning checklist

Water change? ☐ yes ☐ no   Amount changed: _____

☐ Glass   ☐ Gravel   ☐ Top   ☐ Other _____

Maintenance Checklist

notes

☐ Filters   ☐ rinse   ☐ replace   _____

☐ Pumps   _____

☐ Tubing   _____

☐ Connections   _____

☐ Airstones   _____

☐ Skimmers, etc.   _____

☐ Lighting   _____

Restock (food, treatments, equipment, etc.):

_____

_____

Additional Notes:

Date: _____ Tank name/ID: _____

Data

Water level:	_____	Ammonia level:	_____
Temperature:	_____	Nitrite level:	_____
pH level:	_____	Nitrate level:	_____
Alkalinity:	_____	Salinity:	_____
Calcium level:	_____	Phosphate level:	_____
Iodine level:	_____	Magnesium level:	_____

Cleaning checklist

Water change? ☐ yes ☐ no   Amount changed: _____

☐ Glass   ☐ Gravel   ☐ Top   ☐ Other _____

Maintenance Checklist

notes

☐ Filters   ☐ rinse   ☐ replace   _____

☐ Pumps   _____

☐ Tubing   _____

☐ Connections   _____

☐ Airstones   _____

☐ Skimmers, etc.   _____

☐ Lighting   _____

Restock (food, treatments, equipment, etc.):

_____

_____

Additional Notes:

Date: _____   Tank name/ID: _____

Data

Water level:	_____	Ammonia level:	_____
Temperature:	_____	Nitrite level:	_____
pH level:	_____	Nitrate level:	_____
Alkalinity:	_____	Salinity:	_____
Calcium level:	_____	Phosphate level:	_____
Iodine level:	_____	Magnesium level:	_____

Cleaning checklist

Water change? ☐ yes ☐ no   Amount changed: _____

☐ Glass   ☐ Gravel   ☐ Top   ☐ Other _____

Maintenance Checklist

notes

☐ Filters   ☐ rinse   ☐ replace   _____

☐ Pumps   _____

☐ Tubing   _____

☐ Connections   _____

☐ Airstones   _____

☐ Skimmers, etc.   _____

☐ Lighting   _____

Restock (food, treatments, equipment, etc.):

_____

_____

Additional Notes:

Date: _____   Tank name/ID: _____

Data

Water level:	_____	Ammonia level:	_____
Temperature:	_____	Nitrite level:	_____
pH level:	_____	Nitrate level:	_____
Alkalinity:	_____	Salinity:	_____
Calcium level:	_____	Phosphate level:	_____
Iodine level:	_____	Magnesium level:	_____

Cleaning checklist

Water change? ☐ yes ☐ no   Amount changed: _____

☐ Glass   ☐ Gravel   ☐ Top   ☐ Other _____

Maintenance Checklist

notes

☐ Filters   ☐ rinse   ☐ replace   _____

☐ Pumps   _____

☐ Tubing   _____

☐ Connections   _____

☐ Airstones   _____

☐ Skimmers, etc.   _____

☐ Lighting   _____

Restock (food, treatments, equipment, etc.):

_____

_____

Additional Notes:

Date: _____ Tank name/ID: _____

Data

Water level:	_____	Ammonia level:	_____
Temperature:	_____	Nitrite level:	_____
pH level:	_____	Nitrate level:	_____
Alkalinity:	_____	Salinity:	_____
Calcium level:	_____	Phosphate level:	_____
Iodine level:	_____	Magnesium level:	_____

Cleaning checklist

Water change? ☐ yes ☐ no   Amount changed: _____

☐ Glass   ☐ Gravel   ☐ Top   ☐ Other _____

Maintenance Checklist

notes

☐ Filters   ☐ rinse   ☐ replace   _____

☐ Pumps   _____

☐ Tubing   _____

☐ Connections   _____

☐ Airstones   _____

☐ Skimmers, etc.   _____

☐ Lighting   _____

Restock (food, treatments, equipment, etc.):

_____

_____

Additional Notes:

Date: _____   Tank name/ID: _____

Data

Water level:	_____	Ammonia level:	_____
Temperature:	_____	Nitrite level:	_____
pH level:	_____	Nitrate level:	_____
Alkalinity:	_____	Salinity:	_____
Calcium level:	_____	Phosphate level:	_____
Iodine level:	_____	Magnesium level:	_____

Cleaning checklist

Water change? ☐ yes ☐ no   Amount changed: _____

☐ Glass   ☐ Gravel   ☐ Top   ☐ Other _____

Maintenance Checklist

notes

☐ Filters   ☐ rinse   ☐ replace   _____

☐ Pumps   _____

☐ Tubing   _____

☐ Connections   _____

☐ Airstones   _____

☐ Skimmers, etc.   _____

☐ Lighting   _____

Restock (food, treatments, equipment, etc.):

_____

_____

Additional Notes:

Date: Tank name/ID:

Data

Water level:	_____	Ammonia level:	_____
Temperature:	_____	Nitrite level:	_____
pH level:	_____	Nitrate level:	_____
Alkalinity:	_____	Salinity:	_____
Calcium level:	_____	Phosphate level:	_____
Iodine level:	_____	Magnesium level:	_____

Cleaning checklist

Water change? ☐ yes ☐ no   Amount changed: _____

☐ Glass   ☐ Gravel   ☐ Top   ☐ Other _____

Maintenance Checklist

notes

☐ Filters   ☐ rinse   ☐ replace   _____
☐ Pumps   _____
☐ Tubing   _____
☐ Connections   _____
☐ Airstones   _____
☐ Skimmers, etc.   _____
☐ Lighting   _____

Restock (food, treatments, equipment, etc.):

_____
_____

Additional Notes:

Date: _____   Tank name/ID: _____

Data

Water level:	_____	Ammonia level:	_____
Temperature:	_____	Nitrite level:	_____
pH level:	_____	Nitrate level:	_____
Alkalinity:	_____	Salinity:	_____
Calcium level:	_____	Phosphate level:	_____
Iodine level:	_____	Magnesium level:	_____

Cleaning checklist

Water change? ☐ yes ☐ no   Amount changed: _____

☐ Glass   ☐ Gravel   ☐ Top   ☐ Other _____

Maintenance Checklist

notes

☐ Filters   ☐ rinse   ☐ replace   _____
☐ Pumps   _____
☐ Tubing   _____
☐ Connections   _____
☐ Airstones   _____
☐ Skimmers, etc.   _____
☐ Lighting   _____

Restock (food, treatments, equipment, etc.):

_____

_____

Additional Notes:

Date: Tank name/ID:

Data

Water level:	_____	Ammonia level:	_____
Temperature:	_____	Nitrite level:	_____
pH level:	_____	Nitrate level:	_____
Alkalinity:	_____	Salinity:	_____
Calcium level:	_____	Phosphate level:	_____
Iodine level:	_____	Magnesium level:	_____

Cleaning checklist

Water change? ☐ yes ☐ no   Amount changed: _____

☐ Glass   ☐ Gravel   ☐ Top   ☐ Other _____

Maintenance Checklist

<u>notes</u>

☐ Filters   ☐ rinse   ☐ replace   _____

☐ Pumps   _____

☐ Tubing   _____

☐ Connections   _____

☐ Airstones   _____

☐ Skimmers, etc.   _____

☐ Lighting   _____

Restock (food, treatments, equipment, etc.):

_____

_____

Additional Notes:

Date: _____   Tank name/ID: _____

Data

Water level:	_____	Ammonia level:	_____
Temperature:	_____	Nitrite level:	_____
pH level:	_____	Nitrate level:	_____
Alkalinity:	_____	Salinity:	_____
Calcium level:	_____	Phosphate level:	_____
Iodine level:	_____	Magnesium level:	_____

Cleaning checklist

Water change? ☐ yes ☐ no   Amount changed: _____

☐ Glass   ☐ Gravel   ☐ Top   ☐ Other _____

Maintenance Checklist

notes

☐ Filters   ☐ rinse   ☐ replace   _____

☐ Pumps   _____

☐ Tubing   _____

☐ Connections _____

☐ Airstones _____

☐ Skimmers, etc. _____

☐ Lighting   _____

Restock (food, treatments, equipment, etc.):

_____

_____

Additional Notes:

Date: Tank name/ID:

Data

Water level: _____   Ammonia level: _____

Temperature: _____   Nitrite level: _____

pH level: _____   Nitrate level: _____

Alkalinity: _____   Salinity: _____

Calcium level: _____   Phosphate level: _____

Iodine level: _____   Magnesium level: _____

Cleaning checklist

Water change? ☐ yes ☐ no   Amount changed: _____

☐ Glass   ☐ Gravel   ☐ Top   ☐ Other _____

Maintenance Checklist

notes

☐ Filters   ☐ rinse   ☐ replace   _____

☐ Pumps   _____

☐ Tubing   _____

☐ Connections   _____

☐ Airstones   _____

☐ Skimmers, etc.   _____

☐ Lighting   _____

Restock (food, treatments, equipment, etc.):

_____

_____

Additional Notes:

Date: _____ Tank name/ID: _____

Data

Water level:	_____	Ammonia level:	_____
Temperature:	_____	Nitrite level:	_____
pH level:	_____	Nitrate level:	_____
Alkalinity:	_____	Salinity:	_____
Calcium level:	_____	Phosphate level:	_____
Iodine level:	_____	Magnesium level:	_____

Cleaning checklist

Water change? ☐ yes ☐ no   Amount changed: _____

☐ Glass   ☐ Gravel   ☐ Top   ☐ Other _____

Maintenance Checklist

notes

☐ Filters   ☐ rinse   ☐ replace   _____

☐ Pumps   _____

☐ Tubing   _____

☐ Connections   _____

☐ Airstones   _____

☐ Skimmers, etc.   _____

☐ Lighting   _____

Restock (food, treatments, equipment, etc.):

_____

_____

Additional Notes:

Date: _____ Tank name/ID: _____

Data

Water level:	_____	Ammonia level:	_____
Temperature:	_____	Nitrite level:	_____
pH level:	_____	Nitrate level:	_____
Alkalinity:	_____	Salinity:	_____
Calcium level:	_____	Phosphate level:	_____
Iodine level:	_____	Magnesium level:	_____

Cleaning checklist

Water change? ☐ yes ☐ no   Amount changed: _____

☐ Glass   ☐ Gravel   ☐ Top   ☐ Other _____

Maintenance Checklist

notes

☐ Filters   ☐ rinse   ☐ replace   _____

☐ Pumps   _____

☐ Tubing   _____

☐ Connections   _____

☐ Airstones   _____

☐ Skimmers, etc.   _____

☐ Lighting   _____

Restock (food, treatments, equipment, etc.):

_____

_____

Additional Notes:

Date: _____   Tank name/ID: _____

Data

Water level:	_____	Ammonia level:	_____
Temperature:	_____	Nitrite level:	_____
pH level:	_____	Nitrate level:	_____
Alkalinity:	_____	Salinity:	_____
Calcium level:	_____	Phosphate level:	_____
Iodine level:	_____	Magnesium level:	_____

Cleaning checklist

Water change? ☐ yes ☐ no   Amount changed: _____

☐ Glass   ☐ Gravel   ☐ Top   ☐ Other _____

Maintenance Checklist

notes

☐ Filters   ☐ rinse   ☐ replace   _____

☐ Pumps   _____

☐ Tubing   _____

☐ Connections   _____

☐ Airstones   _____

☐ Skimmers, etc.   _____

☐ Lighting   _____

Restock (food, treatments, equipment, etc.):

_____

_____

Additional Notes:

Date: Tank name/ID:

Data

Water level: _____   Ammonia level: _____

Temperature: _____   Nitrite level: _____

pH level: _____   Nitrate level: _____

Alkalinity: _____   Salinity: _____

Calcium level: _____   Phosphate level: _____

Iodine level: _____   Magnesium level: _____

Cleaning checklist

Water change? ☐ yes ☐ no   Amount changed: _____

☐ Glass   ☐ Gravel   ☐ Top   ☐ Other _____

Maintenance Checklist

notes

☐ Filters   ☐ rinse   ☐ replace   _____
☐ Pumps   _____
☐ Tubing   _____
☐ Connections   _____
☐ Airstones   _____
☐ Skimmers, etc.   _____
☐ Lighting   _____

Restock (food, treatments, equipment, etc.):

_____
_____

Additional Notes:

Date: Tank name/ID:

Data

Water level:	_____	Ammonia level:	_____
Temperature:	_____	Nitrite level:	_____
pH level:	_____	Nitrate level:	_____
Alkalinity:	_____	Salinity:	_____
Calcium level:	_____	Phosphate level:	_____
Iodine level:	_____	Magnesium level:	_____

Cleaning checklist

Water change? ☐ yes ☐ no   Amount changed: _____

☐ Glass   ☐ Gravel   ☐ Top   ☐ Other _____

Maintenance Checklist

notes

☐ Filters   ☐ rinse   ☐ replace   _____
☐ Pumps   _____
☐ Tubing   _____
☐ Connections   _____
☐ Airstones   _____
☐ Skimmers, etc.   _____
☐ Lighting   _____

Restock (food, treatments, equipment, etc.):

_____

_____

Additional Notes:

Date: _____ Tank name/ID: _____

Data

Water level:	_____	Ammonia level:	_____
Temperature:	_____	Nitrite level:	_____
pH level:	_____	Nitrate level:	_____
Alkalinity:	_____	Salinity:	_____
Calcium level:	_____	Phosphate level:	_____
Iodine level:	_____	Magnesium level:	_____

Cleaning checklist

Water change? ☐ yes ☐ no   Amount changed: _____

☐ Glass   ☐ Gravel   ☐ Top   ☐ Other _____

Maintenance Checklist

notes

☐ Filters   ☐ rinse   ☐ replace   _____

☐ Pumps   _____

☐ Tubing   _____

☐ Connections   _____

☐ Airstones   _____

☐ Skimmers, etc.   _____

☐ Lighting   _____

Restock (food, treatments, equipment, etc.):

_____

_____

Additional Notes:

Date: _____   Tank name/ID: _____

Data

Water level: _____   Ammonia level: _____

Temperature: _____   Nitrite level: _____

pH level: _____   Nitrate level: _____

Alkalinity: _____   Salinity: _____

Calcium level: _____   Phosphate level: _____

Iodine level: _____   Magnesium level: _____

Cleaning checklist

Water change? ☐ yes ☐ no   Amount changed: _____

☐ Glass   ☐ Gravel   ☐ Top   ☐ Other _____

Maintenance Checklist

notes

☐ Filters   ☐ rinse   ☐ replace   _____

☐ Pumps   _____

☐ Tubing   _____

☐ Connections   _____

☐ Airstones   _____

☐ Skimmers, etc.   _____

☐ Lighting   _____

Restock (food, treatments, equipment, etc.):

_____

_____

Additional Notes:

Date: _____   Tank name/ID: _____

Data

Water level:	_____	Ammonia level:	_____
Temperature:	_____	Nitrite level:	_____
pH level:	_____	Nitrate level:	_____
Alkalinity:	_____	Salinity:	_____
Calcium level:	_____	Phosphate level:	_____
Iodine level:	_____	Magnesium level:	_____

Cleaning checklist

Water change? ☐ yes ☐ no   Amount changed: _____

☐ Glass   ☐ Gravel   ☐ Top   ☐ Other _____

Maintenance Checklist

notes

☐ Filters   ☐ rinse   ☐ replace   _____

☐ Pumps   _____

☐ Tubing   _____

☐ Connections   _____

☐ Airstones   _____

☐ Skimmers, etc.   _____

☐ Lighting   _____

Restock (food, treatments, equipment, etc.):

_____

_____

Additional Notes:

Date: Tank name/ID:

Data

Water level: _____   Ammonia level: _____

Temperature: _____   Nitrite level: _____

pH level: _____   Nitrate level: _____

Alkalinity: _____   Salinity: _____

Calcium level: _____   Phosphate level: _____

Iodine level: _____   Magnesium level: _____

Cleaning checklist

Water change? ☐ yes ☐ no   Amount changed: _____

☐ Glass   ☐ Gravel   ☐ Top   ☐ Other _____

Maintenance Checklist

notes

☐ Filters   ☐ rinse   ☐ replace   _____
☐ Pumps   _____
☐ Tubing   _____
☐ Connections   _____
☐ Airstones   _____
☐ Skimmers, etc.   _____
☐ Lighting   _____

Restock (food, treatments, equipment, etc.):

_____
_____

Additional Notes:

Date: Tank name/ID:

Data

Water level: _____   Ammonia level: _____

Temperature: _____   Nitrite level: _____

pH level: _____   Nitrate level: _____

Alkalinity: _____   Salinity: _____

Calcium level: _____   Phosphate level: _____

Iodine level: _____   Magnesium level: _____

Cleaning checklist

Water change? ☐ yes ☐ no   Amount changed: _____

☐ Glass   ☐ Gravel   ☐ Top   ☐ Other _____

Maintenance Checklist

<u>notes</u>

☐ Filters   ☐ rinse   ☐ replace   _____

☐ Pumps   _____

☐ Tubing   _____

☐ Connections   _____

☐ Airstones   _____

☐ Skimmers, etc.   _____

☐ Lighting   _____

Restock (food, treatments, equipment, etc.):

_____

_____

Additional Notes:

Date: Tank name/ID:

Data

Water level: _____ Ammonia level: _____

Temperature: _____ Nitrite level: _____

pH level: _____ Nitrate level: _____

Alkalinity: _____ Salinity: _____

Calcium level: _____ Phosphate level: _____

Iodine level: _____ Magnesium level: _____

Cleaning checklist

Water change? ☐ yes ☐ no   Amount changed: _____

☐ Glass ☐ Gravel ☐ Top ☐ Other _____

Maintenance Checklist

<u>notes</u>

☐ Filters ☐ rinse ☐ replace _____

☐ Pumps _____

☐ Tubing _____

☐ Connections _____

☐ Airstones _____

☐ Skimmers, etc. _____

☐ Lighting _____

Restock (food, treatments, equipment, etc.):

_____

_____

Additional Notes:

Date: _____ Tank name/ID: _____

Data

Water level:	_____	Ammonia level:	_____
Temperature:	_____	Nitrite level:	_____
pH level:	_____	Nitrate level:	_____
Alkalinity:	_____	Salinity:	_____
Calcium level:	_____	Phosphate level:	_____
Iodine level:	_____	Magnesium level:	_____

Cleaning checklist

Water change? ☐ yes ☐ no   Amount changed: _____

☐ Glass   ☐ Gravel   ☐ Top   ☐ Other _____

Maintenance Checklist

notes

☐ Filters   ☐ rinse   ☐ replace   _____

☐ Pumps   _____

☐ Tubing   _____

☐ Connections   _____

☐ Airstones   _____

☐ Skimmers, etc.   _____

☐ Lighting   _____

Restock (food, treatments, equipment, etc.):

_____

_____

Additional Notes:

Date: _____   Tank name/ID: _____

Data

Water level: _____   Ammonia level: _____

Temperature: _____   Nitrite level: _____

pH level: _____   Nitrate level: _____

Alkalinity: _____   Salinity: _____

Calcium level: _____   Phosphate level: _____

Iodine level: _____   Magnesium level: _____

Cleaning checklist

Water change? ☐ yes ☐ no   Amount changed: _____

☐ Glass   ☐ Gravel   ☐ Top   ☐ Other _____

Maintenance Checklist

notes

☐ Filters   ☐ rinse   ☐ replace   _____

☐ Pumps   _____

☐ Tubing   _____

☐ Connections   _____

☐ Airstones   _____

☐ Skimmers, etc.   _____

☐ Lighting   _____

Restock (food, treatments, equipment, etc.):

_____

_____

Additional Notes:

Date: Tank name/ID:

Data

Water level:	_____	Ammonia level:	_____
Temperature:	_____	Nitrite level:	_____
pH level:	_____	Nitrate level:	_____
Alkalinity:	_____	Salinity:	_____
Calcium level:	_____	Phosphate level:	_____
Iodine level:	_____	Magnesium level:	_____

Cleaning checklist

Water change? ☐ yes ☐ no   Amount changed: _____

☐ Glass   ☐ Gravel   ☐ Top   ☐ Other _____

Maintenance Checklist

notes

☐ Filters   ☐ rinse   ☐ replace   _____

☐ Pumps   _____

☐ Tubing   _____

☐ Connections   _____

☐ Airstones   _____

☐ Skimmers, etc.   _____

☐ Lighting   _____

Restock (food, treatments, equipment, etc.):

_____

_____

Additional Notes:

Date: Tank name/ID:

Data

Water level:	_____	Ammonia level:	_____
Temperature:	_____	Nitrite level:	_____
pH level:	_____	Nitrate level:	_____
Alkalinity:	_____	Salinity:	_____
Calcium level:	_____	Phosphate level:	_____
Iodine level:	_____	Magnesium level:	_____

Cleaning checklist

Water change? ☐ yes ☐ no   Amount changed: _____

☐ Glass   ☐ Gravel   ☐ Top   ☐ Other _____

Maintenance Checklist

notes

☐ Filters   ☐ rinse   ☐ replace   _____

☐ Pumps   _____

☐ Tubing   _____

☐ Connections   _____

☐ Airstones   _____

☐ Skimmers, etc.   _____

☐ Lighting   _____

Restock (food, treatments, equipment, etc.):

_____

_____

Additional Notes:

Date: Tank name/ID:

Data

Water level:	_____	Ammonia level:	_____
Temperature:	_____	Nitrite level:	_____
pH level:	_____	Nitrate level:	_____
Alkalinity:	_____	Salinity:	_____
Calcium level:	_____	Phosphate level:	_____
Iodine level:	_____	Magnesium level:	_____

Cleaning checklist

Water change? ☐ yes ☐ no   Amount changed: _____

☐ Glass   ☐ Gravel   ☐ Top   ☐ Other _____

Maintenance Checklist

notes

☐ Filters   ☐ rinse   ☐ replace   _____

☐ Pumps   _____

☐ Tubing   _____

☐ Connections   _____

☐ Airstones   _____

☐ Skimmers, etc.   _____

☐ Lighting   _____

Restock (food, treatments, equipment, etc.):

_____

_____

Additional Notes:

Date: _____   Tank name/ID: _____

Data

Water level: _____   Ammonia level: _____

Temperature: _____   Nitrite level: _____

pH level: _____   Nitrate level: _____

Alkalinity: _____   Salinity: _____

Calcium level: _____   Phosphate level: _____

Iodine level: _____   Magnesium level: _____

Cleaning checklist

Water change? ☐ yes ☐ no   Amount changed: _____

☐ Glass   ☐ Gravel   ☐ Top   ☐ Other _____

Maintenance Checklist

notes

☐ Filters   ☐ rinse   ☐ replace   _____

☐ Pumps   _____

☐ Tubing   _____

☐ Connections   _____

☐ Airstones   _____

☐ Skimmers, etc.   _____

☐ Lighting   _____

Restock (food, treatments, equipment, etc.):

_____

_____

Additional Notes:

Date: _____ Tank name/ID: _____

Data

Water level: _____ Ammonia level: _____

Temperature: _____ Nitrite level: _____

pH level: _____ Nitrate level: _____

Alkalinity: _____ Salinity: _____

Calcium level: _____ Phosphate level: _____

Iodine level: _____ Magnesium level: _____

Cleaning checklist

Water change? ☐ yes ☐ no   Amount changed: _____

☐ Glass ☐ Gravel ☐ Top ☐ Other _____

Maintenance Checklist

notes

☐ Filters ☐ rinse ☐ replace _____

☐ Pumps _____

☐ Tubing _____

☐ Connections _____

☐ Airstones _____

☐ Skimmers, etc. _____

☐ Lighting _____

Restock (food, treatments, equipment, etc.):

_____

_____

Additional Notes:

Date: Tank name/ID:

Data

Water level:	_____	Ammonia level:	_____
Temperature:	_____	Nitrite level:	_____
pH level:	_____	Nitrate level:	_____
Alkalinity:	_____	Salinity:	_____
Calcium level:	_____	Phosphate level:	_____
Iodine level:	_____	Magnesium level:	_____

Cleaning checklist

Water change? ☐ yes ☐ no   Amount changed: _____

☐ Glass   ☐ Gravel   ☐ Top   ☐ Other _____

Maintenance Checklist

notes

☐ Filters   ☐ rinse   ☐ replace   _____

☐ Pumps   _____

☐ Tubing   _____

☐ Connections   _____

☐ Airstones   _____

☐ Skimmers, etc.   _____

☐ Lighting   _____

Restock (food, treatments, equipment, etc.):

_____

_____

Additional Notes:

Date: _____   Tank name/ID: _____

Data

Water level: _____   Ammonia level: _____

Temperature: _____   Nitrite level: _____

pH level: _____   Nitrate level: _____

Alkalinity: _____   Salinity: _____

Calcium level: _____   Phosphate level: _____

Iodine level: _____   Magnesium level: _____

Cleaning checklist

Water change? ☐ yes ☐ no   Amount changed: _____

☐ Glass   ☐ Gravel   ☐ Top   ☐ Other _____

Maintenance Checklist

notes

☐ Filters   ☐ rinse   ☐ replace   _____

☐ Pumps   _____

☐ Tubing   _____

☐ Connections   _____

☐ Airstones   _____

☐ Skimmers, etc.   _____

☐ Lighting   _____

Restock (food, treatments, equipment, etc.):

_____

_____

Additional Notes:

Date: Tank name/ID:

Data

Water level:	_____	Ammonia level:	_____
Temperature:	_____	Nitrite level:	_____
pH level:	_____	Nitrate level:	_____
Alkalinity:	_____	Salinity:	_____
Calcium level:	_____	Phosphate level:	_____
Iodine level:	_____	Magnesium level:	_____

Cleaning checklist

Water change? ☐ yes ☐ no   Amount changed: _____

☐ Glass   ☐ Gravel   ☐ Top   ☐ Other _____

Maintenance Checklist

<u>notes</u>

☐ Filters   ☐ rinse   ☐ replace   _____

☐ Pumps   _____

☐ Tubing   _____

☐ Connections   _____

☐ Airstones   _____

☐ Skimmers, etc.   _____

☐ Lighting   _____

Restock (food, treatments, equipment, etc.):

_____

_____

Additional Notes:

Date: _____ Tank name/ID: _____

Data

Water level:	_____	Ammonia level:	_____
Temperature:	_____	Nitrite level:	_____
pH level:	_____	Nitrate level:	_____
Alkalinity:	_____	Salinity:	_____
Calcium level:	_____	Phosphate level:	_____
Iodine level:	_____	Magnesium level:	_____

Cleaning checklist

Water change? ☐ yes ☐ no   Amount changed: _____

☐ Glass   ☐ Gravel   ☐ Top   ☐ Other _____

Maintenance Checklist

notes

☐ Filters   ☐ rinse   ☐ replace   _____
☐ Pumps   _____
☐ Tubing   _____
☐ Connections   _____
☐ Airstones   _____
☐ Skimmers, etc.   _____
☐ Lighting   _____

Restock (food, treatments, equipment, etc.):

_____

_____

Additional Notes:

Date: Tank name/ID:

Data

Water level:	_____	Ammonia level:	_____
Temperature:	_____	Nitrite level:	_____
pH level:	_____	Nitrate level:	_____
Alkalinity:	_____	Salinity:	_____
Calcium level:	_____	Phosphate level:	_____
Iodine level:	_____	Magnesium level:	_____

Cleaning checklist

Water change? ☐ yes ☐ no   Amount changed: _____

☐ Glass   ☐ Gravel   ☐ Top   ☐ Other _____

Maintenance Checklist

notes

☐ Filters   ☐ rinse   ☐ replace   _____

☐ Pumps   _____

☐ Tubing   _____

☐ Connections   _____

☐ Airstones   _____

☐ Skimmers, etc.   _____

☐ Lighting   _____

Restock (food, treatments, equipment, etc.):

_____

_____

Additional Notes:

Date: _____   Tank name/ID: _____

Data

Water level: _____   Ammonia level: _____

Temperature: _____   Nitrite level: _____

pH level: _____   Nitrate level: _____

Alkalinity: _____   Salinity: _____

Calcium level: _____   Phosphate level: _____

Iodine level: _____   Magnesium level: _____

Cleaning checklist

Water change? ☐ yes ☐ no   Amount changed: _____

☐ Glass   ☐ Gravel   ☐ Top   ☐ Other _____

Maintenance Checklist

notes

☐ Filters   ☐ rinse   ☐ replace   _____

☐ Pumps   _____

☐ Tubing   _____

☐ Connections   _____

☐ Airstones   _____

☐ Skimmers, etc.   _____

☐ Lighting   _____

Restock (food, treatments, equipment, etc.):

_____

_____

Additional Notes:

Date: Tank name/ID:

Data

Water level: _____ Ammonia level: _____

Temperature: _____ Nitrite level: _____

pH level: _____ Nitrate level: _____

Alkalinity: _____ Salinity: _____

Calcium level: _____ Phosphate level: _____

Iodine level: _____ Magnesium level: _____

Cleaning checklist

Water change? ☐ yes ☐ no   Amount changed: _____

☐ Glass   ☐ Gravel   ☐ Top   ☐ Other _____

Maintenance Checklist

notes

☐ Filters   ☐ rinse   ☐ replace   _____

☐ Pumps   _____

☐ Tubing   _____

☐ Connections   _____

☐ Airstones   _____

☐ Skimmers, etc.   _____

☐ Lighting   _____

Restock (food, treatments, equipment, etc.):

_____

_____

Additional Notes:

Date: Tank name/ID:

Data

Water level:	_____	Ammonia level:	_____
Temperature:	_____	Nitrite level:	_____
pH level:	_____	Nitrate level:	_____
Alkalinity:	_____	Salinity:	_____
Calcium level:	_____	Phosphate level:	_____
Iodine level:	_____	Magnesium level:	_____

Cleaning checklist

Water change? ☐ yes ☐ no   Amount changed: _____

☐ Glass   ☐ Gravel   ☐ Top   ☐ Other _____

Maintenance Checklist

notes

☐ Filters   ☐ rinse   ☐ replace   _____

☐ Pumps   _____

☐ Tubing   _____

☐ Connections   _____

☐ Airstones   _____

☐ Skimmers, etc.   _____

☐ Lighting   _____

Restock (food, treatments, equipment, etc.):

_____

_____

Additional Notes:

Date: Tank name/ID:

Data

Water level:	_____	Ammonia level:	_____
Temperature:	_____	Nitrite level:	_____
pH level:	_____	Nitrate level:	_____
Alkalinity:	_____	Salinity:	_____
Calcium level:	_____	Phosphate level:	_____
Iodine level:	_____	Magnesium level:	_____

Cleaning checklist

Water change? ☐ yes ☐ no   Amount changed: _____

☐ Glass   ☐ Gravel   ☐ Top   ☐ Other _____

Maintenance Checklist

notes

☐ Filters   ☐ rinse   ☐ replace   _____

☐ Pumps   _____

☐ Tubing   _____

☐ Connections   _____

☐ Airstones   _____

☐ Skimmers, etc.   _____

☐ Lighting   _____

Restock (food, treatments, equipment, etc.):

_____

_____

Additional Notes:

Date: _____   Tank name/ID: _____

Data

Water level:	_____	Ammonia level:	_____
Temperature:	_____	Nitrite level:	_____
pH level:	_____	Nitrate level:	_____
Alkalinity:	_____	Salinity:	_____
Calcium level:	_____	Phosphate level:	_____
Iodine level:	_____	Magnesium level:	_____

Cleaning checklist

Water change? ☐ yes ☐ no   Amount changed: _____

☐ Glass   ☐ Gravel   ☐ Top   ☐ Other _____

Maintenance Checklist

notes

☐ Filters   ☐ rinse   ☐ replace   _____
☐ Pumps   _____
☐ Tubing   _____
☐ Connections   _____
☐ Airstones   _____
☐ Skimmers, etc.   _____
☐ Lighting   _____

Restock (food, treatments, equipment, etc.):

_____
_____

Additional Notes:

Date: Tank name/ID:

Data

Water level:	_____	Ammonia level:	_____
Temperature:	_____	Nitrite level:	_____
pH level:	_____	Nitrate level:	_____
Alkalinity:	_____	Salinity:	_____
Calcium level:	_____	Phosphate level:	_____
Iodine level:	_____	Magnesium level:	_____

Cleaning checklist

Water change? ☐ yes ☐ no   Amount changed: _____

☐ Glass   ☐ Gravel   ☐ Top   ☐ Other _____

Maintenance Checklist

notes

☐ Filters   ☐ rinse   ☐ replace   _____

☐ Pumps   _____

☐ Tubing   _____

☐ Connections   _____

☐ Airstones   _____

☐ Skimmers, etc.   _____

☐ Lighting   _____

Restock (food, treatments, equipment, etc.):

_____

_____

Additional Notes:

Date: _____ Tank name/ID: _____

Data

Water level:	_____	Ammonia level:	_____
Temperature:	_____	Nitrite level:	_____
pH level:	_____	Nitrate level:	_____
Alkalinity:	_____	Salinity:	_____
Calcium level:	_____	Phosphate level:	_____
Iodine level:	_____	Magnesium level:	_____

Cleaning checklist

Water change? ☐ yes ☐ no   Amount changed: _____

☐ Glass   ☐ Gravel   ☐ Top   ☐ Other _____

Maintenance Checklist

notes

☐ Filters ☐ rinse ☐ replace _____

☐ Pumps _____

☐ Tubing _____

☐ Connections _____

☐ Airstones _____

☐ Skimmers, etc. _____

☐ Lighting _____

Restock (food, treatments, equipment, etc.):

_____

_____

Additional Notes:

Date: _____ Tank name/ID: _____

Data

Water level:	_____	Ammonia level:	_____
Temperature:	_____	Nitrite level:	_____
pH level:	_____	Nitrate level:	_____
Alkalinity:	_____	Salinity:	_____
Calcium level:	_____	Phosphate level:	_____
Iodine level:	_____	Magnesium level:	_____

Cleaning checklist

Water change? ☐ yes ☐ no   Amount changed: _____

☐ Glass   ☐ Gravel   ☐ Top   ☐ Other _____

Maintenance Checklist

notes

☐ Filters   ☐ rinse   ☐ replace   _____
☐ Pumps   _____
☐ Tubing   _____
☐ Connections   _____
☐ Airstones   _____
☐ Skimmers, etc.   _____
☐ Lighting   _____

Restock (food, treatments, equipment, etc.):

_____

_____

Additional Notes:

Date: Tank name/ID:

Data

Water level:	_____	Ammonia level:	_____
Temperature:	_____	Nitrite level:	_____
pH level:	_____	Nitrate level:	_____
Alkalinity:	_____	Salinity:	_____
Calcium level:	_____	Phosphate level:	_____
Iodine level:	_____	Magnesium level:	_____

Cleaning checklist

Water change? ☐ yes ☐ no   Amount changed: _____

☐ Glass   ☐ Gravel   ☐ Top   ☐ Other _____

Maintenance Checklist

notes

☐ Filters   ☐ rinse   ☐ replace   _____

☐ Pumps   _____

☐ Tubing   _____

☐ Connections   _____

☐ Airstones   _____

☐ Skimmers, etc.   _____

☐ Lighting   _____

Restock (food, treatments, equipment, etc.):

_____

_____

Additional Notes:

Date: _____   Tank name/ID: _____

Data

Water level: _____   Ammonia level: _____

Temperature: _____   Nitrite level: _____

pH level: _____   Nitrate level: _____

Alkalinity: _____   Salinity: _____

Calcium level: _____   Phosphate level: _____

Iodine level: _____   Magnesium level: _____

Cleaning checklist

Water change? ☐ yes ☐ no   Amount changed: _____

☐ Glass   ☐ Gravel   ☐ Top   ☐ Other _____

Maintenance Checklist

notes

☐ Filters   ☐ rinse   ☐ replace   _____

☐ Pumps   _____

☐ Tubing   _____

☐ Connections _____

☐ Airstones   _____

☐ Skimmers, etc. _____

☐ Lighting   _____

Restock (food, treatments, equipment, etc.):

_____

_____

Additional Notes:

Date: Tank name/ID:

Data

Water level: _____   Ammonia level: _____

Temperature: _____   Nitrite level: _____

pH level: _____   Nitrate level: _____

Alkalinity: _____   Salinity: _____

Calcium level: _____   Phosphate level: _____

Iodine level: _____   Magnesium level: _____

Cleaning checklist

Water change?   ☐ yes   ☐ no   Amount changed: _____

☐   Glass   ☐   Gravel   ☐   Top   ☐   Other _____

Maintenance Checklist

<u>notes</u>

☐   Filters   ☐ rinse   ☐ replace   _____

☐   Pumps   _____

☐   Tubing   _____

☐   Connections   _____

☐   Airstones   _____

☐   Skimmers, etc.   _____

☐   Lighting   _____

Restock (food, treatments, equipment, etc.):

_____

_____

Additional Notes:

Date: Tank name/ID:

Data

Water level: _____ Ammonia level: _____

Temperature: _____ Nitrite level: _____

pH level: _____ Nitrate level: _____

Alkalinity: _____ Salinity: _____

Calcium level: _____ Phosphate level: _____

Iodine level: _____ Magnesium level: _____

Cleaning checklist

Water change? ☐ yes ☐ no   Amount changed: _____

☐ Glass   ☐ Gravel   ☐ Top   ☐ Other _____

Maintenance Checklist

notes

☐ Filters   ☐ rinse   ☐ replace   _____
☐ Pumps   _____
☐ Tubing   _____
☐ Connections   _____
☐ Airstones   _____
☐ Skimmers, etc.   _____
☐ Lighting   _____

Restock (food, treatments, equipment, etc.):

_____
_____

Additional Notes:

Date: Tank name/ID:

Data

Water level:	_____	Ammonia level:	_____
Temperature:	_____	Nitrite level:	_____
pH level:	_____	Nitrate level:	_____
Alkalinity:	_____	Salinity:	_____
Calcium level:	_____	Phosphate level:	_____
Iodine level:	_____	Magnesium level:	_____

Cleaning checklist

Water change? ☐ yes ☐ no   Amount changed: _____

☐ Glass   ☐ Gravel   ☐ Top   ☐ Other _____

Maintenance Checklist

notes

☐ Filters   ☐ rinse   ☐ replace   _____

☐ Pumps   _____

☐ Tubing   _____

☐ Connections   _____

☐ Airstones   _____

☐ Skimmers, etc.   _____

☐ Lighting   _____

Restock (food, treatments, equipment, etc.):

_____

_____

Additional Notes:

Date: Tank name/ID:

Data

Water level: _____   Ammonia level: _____

Temperature: _____   Nitrite level: _____

pH level: _____   Nitrate level: _____

Alkalinity: _____   Salinity: _____

Calcium level: _____   Phosphate level: _____

Iodine level: _____   Magnesium level: _____

Cleaning checklist

Water change? ☐ yes ☐ no   Amount changed: _____

☐ Glass   ☐ Gravel   ☐ Top   ☐ Other _____

Maintenance Checklist

notes

☐ Filters   ☐ rinse   ☐ replace   _____

☐ Pumps   _____

☐ Tubing   _____

☐ Connections   _____

☐ Airstones   _____

☐ Skimmers, etc.   _____

☐ Lighting   _____

Restock (food, treatments, equipment, etc.):

_____

_____

Additional Notes:

Date: Tank name/ID:

Data

Water level:	_____	Ammonia level:	_____
Temperature:	_____	Nitrite level:	_____
pH level:	_____	Nitrate level:	_____
Alkalinity:	_____	Salinity:	_____
Calcium level:	_____	Phosphate level:	_____
Iodine level:	_____	Magnesium level:	_____

Cleaning checklist

Water change? ☐ yes ☐ no   Amount changed: _____

☐ Glass   ☐ Gravel   ☐ Top   ☐ Other _____

Maintenance Checklist

<u>notes</u>

☐ Filters   ☐ rinse   ☐ replace   _____

☐ Pumps   _____

☐ Tubing   _____

☐ Connections   _____

☐ Airstones   _____

☐ Skimmers, etc.   _____

☐ Lighting   _____

Restock (food, treatments, equipment, etc.):

_____

_____

Additional Notes:

Date: _____   Tank name/ID: _____

Data

Water level: _____   Ammonia level: _____

Temperature: _____   Nitrite level: _____

pH level: _____   Nitrate level: _____

Alkalinity: _____   Salinity: _____

Calcium level: _____   Phosphate level: _____

Iodine level: _____   Magnesium level: _____

Cleaning checklist

Water change? ☐ yes ☐ no   Amount changed: _____

☐ Glass   ☐ Gravel   ☐ Top   ☐ Other _____

Maintenance Checklist

notes

☐ Filters   ☐ rinse   ☐ replace   _____

☐ Pumps   _____

☐ Tubing   _____

☐ Connections   _____

☐ Airstones   _____

☐ Skimmers, etc.   _____

☐ Lighting   _____

Restock (food, treatments, equipment, etc.):

_____

_____

Additional Notes:

Date: _____ Tank name/ID: _____

Data

Water level:	_____	Ammonia level:	_____
Temperature:	_____	Nitrite level:	_____
pH level:	_____	Nitrate level:	_____
Alkalinity:	_____	Salinity:	_____
Calcium level:	_____	Phosphate level:	_____
Iodine level:	_____	Magnesium level:	_____

Cleaning checklist

Water change? ☐ yes ☐ no   Amount changed: _____

☐ Glass   ☐ Gravel   ☐ Top   ☐ Other _____

Maintenance Checklist

notes

☐ Filters   ☐ rinse   ☐ replace   _____
☐ Pumps   _____
☐ Tubing   _____
☐ Connections   _____
☐ Airstones   _____
☐ Skimmers, etc.   _____
☐ Lighting   _____

Restock (food, treatments, equipment, etc.):

_____

_____

Additional Notes:

Date: Tank name/ID:

Data

Water level: _____   Ammonia level: _____

Temperature: _____   Nitrite level: _____

pH level: _____   Nitrate level: _____

Alkalinity: _____   Salinity: _____

Calcium level: _____   Phosphate level: _____

Iodine level: _____   Magnesium level: _____

Cleaning checklist

Water change? ☐ yes ☐ no   Amount changed: _____

☐ Glass   ☐ Gravel   ☐ Top   ☐ Other _____

Maintenance Checklist

<u>notes</u>

☐ Filters   ☐ rinse   ☐ replace   _____

☐ Pumps   _____

☐ Tubing   _____

☐ Connections   _____

☐ Airstones   _____

☐ Skimmers, etc.   _____

☐ Lighting   _____

Restock (food, treatments, equipment, etc.):

_____

_____

Additional Notes:

Date: _____   Tank name/ID: _____

Data

Water level:	_____	Ammonia level:	_____
Temperature:	_____	Nitrite level:	_____
pH level:	_____	Nitrate level:	_____
Alkalinity:	_____	Salinity:	_____
Calcium level:	_____	Phosphate level:	_____
Iodine level:	_____	Magnesium level:	_____

Cleaning checklist

Water change? ☐ yes ☐ no   Amount changed: _____

☐ Glass   ☐ Gravel   ☐ Top   ☐ Other _____

Maintenance Checklist

notes

☐ Filters   ☐ rinse   ☐ replace   _____
☐ Pumps   _____
☐ Tubing   _____
☐ Connections   _____
☐ Airstones   _____
☐ Skimmers, etc.   _____
☐ Lighting   _____

Restock (food, treatments, equipment, etc.):

_____

_____

Additional Notes:

Date: _____ Tank name/ID: _____

Data

Water level: _____	Ammonia level:	_____
Temperature: _____	Nitrite level:	_____
pH level: _____	Nitrate level:	_____
Alkalinity: _____	Salinity:	_____
Calcium level: _____	Phosphate level:	_____
Iodine level: _____	Magnesium level:	_____

Cleaning checklist

Water change? ☐ yes ☐ no   Amount changed: _____

☐ Glass   ☐ Gravel   ☐ Top   ☐ Other _____

Maintenance Checklist

<u>notes</u>

☐ Filters   ☐ rinse   ☐ replace   _____

☐ Pumps   _____

☐ Tubing   _____

☐ Connections   _____

☐ Airstones   _____

☐ Skimmers, etc.   _____

☐ Lighting   _____

Restock (food, treatments, equipment, etc.):

_____

_____

Additional Notes:

Date: _____ Tank name/ID: _____

Data

Water level:	_____	Ammonia level:	_____
Temperature:	_____	Nitrite level:	_____
pH level:	_____	Nitrate level:	_____
Alkalinity:	_____	Salinity:	_____
Calcium level:	_____	Phosphate level:	_____
Iodine level:	_____	Magnesium level:	_____

Cleaning checklist

Water change? ☐ yes ☐ no   Amount changed: _____

☐ Glass   ☐ Gravel   ☐ Top   ☐ Other _____

Maintenance Checklist

<u>notes</u>

☐ Filters   ☐ rinse   ☐ replace   _____
☐ Pumps   _____
☐ Tubing   _____
☐ Connections   _____
☐ Airstones   _____
☐ Skimmers, etc.   _____
☐ Lighting   _____

Restock (food, treatments, equipment, etc.):

_____
_____

Additional Notes:

Date: Tank name/ID:

Data

Water level:	_____	Ammonia level:	_____
Temperature:	_____	Nitrite level:	_____
pH level:	_____	Nitrate level:	_____
Alkalinity:	_____	Salinity:	_____
Calcium level:	_____	Phosphate level:	_____
Iodine level:	_____	Magnesium level:	_____

Cleaning checklist

Water change? ☐ yes ☐ no   Amount changed: _____

☐ Glass   ☐ Gravel   ☐ Top   ☐ Other _____

Maintenance Checklist

<u>notes</u>

☐ Filters   ☐ rinse   ☐ replace   _____

☐ Pumps   _____

☐ Tubing   _____

☐ Connections   _____

☐ Airstones   _____

☐ Skimmers, etc.   _____

☐ Lighting   _____

Restock (food, treatments, equipment, etc.):

_____

_____

Additional Notes:

Date: _____ Tank name/ID: _____

Data

Water level:	_____	Ammonia level:	_____
Temperature:	_____	Nitrite level:	_____
pH level:	_____	Nitrate level:	_____
Alkalinity:	_____	Salinity:	_____
Calcium level:	_____	Phosphate level:	_____
Iodine level:	_____	Magnesium level:	_____

Cleaning checklist

Water change? ☐ yes ☐ no   Amount changed: _____

☐ Glass   ☐ Gravel   ☐ Top   ☐ Other _____

Maintenance Checklist

notes

☐ Filters   ☐ rinse   ☐ replace   _____
☐ Pumps   _____
☐ Tubing   _____
☐ Connections   _____
☐ Airstones   _____
☐ Skimmers, etc.   _____
☐ Lighting   _____

Restock (food, treatments, equipment, etc.):

_____

_____

Additional Notes:

Date: _____   Tank name/ID: _____

Data

Water level:	_____	Ammonia level:	_____
Temperature:	_____	Nitrite level:	_____
pH level:	_____	Nitrate level:	_____
Alkalinity:	_____	Salinity:	_____
Calcium level:	_____	Phosphate level:	_____
Iodine level:	_____	Magnesium level:	_____

Cleaning checklist

Water change? ☐ yes ☐ no   Amount changed: _____

☐ Glass   ☐ Gravel   ☐ Top   ☐ Other _____

Maintenance Checklist

notes

☐ Filters   ☐ rinse   ☐ replace   _____

☐ Pumps   _____

☐ Tubing   _____

☐ Connections   _____

☐ Airstones   _____

☐ Skimmers, etc. _____

☐ Lighting   _____

Restock (food, treatments, equipment, etc.):

_____

_____

Additional Notes:

Date: _____ Tank name/ID: _____

Data

Water level:	_____	Ammonia level:	_____
Temperature:	_____	Nitrite level:	_____
pH level:	_____	Nitrate level:	_____
Alkalinity:	_____	Salinity:	_____
Calcium level:	_____	Phosphate level:	_____
Iodine level:	_____	Magnesium level:	_____

Cleaning checklist

Water change? ☐ yes ☐ no   Amount changed: _____

☐ Glass   ☐ Gravel   ☐ Top   ☐ Other _____

Maintenance Checklist

notes

☐ Filters   ☐ rinse   ☐ replace   _____
☐ Pumps   _____
☐ Tubing   _____
☐ Connections   _____
☐ Airstones   _____
☐ Skimmers, etc.   _____
☐ Lighting   _____

Restock (food, treatments, equipment, etc.):

_____
_____

Additional Notes:

Date: _____ Tank name/ID: _____

Data

Water level:	_____	Ammonia level:	_____
Temperature:	_____	Nitrite level:	_____
pH level:	_____	Nitrate level:	_____
Alkalinity:	_____	Salinity:	_____
Calcium level:	_____	Phosphate level:	_____
Iodine level:	_____	Magnesium level:	_____

Cleaning checklist

Water change? ☐ yes ☐ no   Amount changed: _____

☐ Glass   ☐ Gravel   ☐ Top   ☐ Other _____

Maintenance Checklist

<u>notes</u>

☐ Filters   ☐ rinse   ☐ replace   _____

☐ Pumps   _____

☐ Tubing   _____

☐ Connections   _____

☐ Airstones   _____

☐ Skimmers, etc.   _____

☐ Lighting   _____

Restock (food, treatments, equipment, etc.):

_____

_____

Additional Notes:

Date: Tank name/ID:

Data

Water level: _____   Ammonia level: _____

Temperature: _____   Nitrite level: _____

pH level: _____   Nitrate level: _____

Alkalinity: _____   Salinity: _____

Calcium level: _____   Phosphate level: _____

Iodine level: _____   Magnesium level: _____

Cleaning checklist

Water change? ☐ yes ☐ no   Amount changed: _____

☐ Glass   ☐ Gravel   ☐ Top   ☐ Other _____

Maintenance Checklist

notes

☐ Filters   ☐ rinse   ☐ replace   _____

☐ Pumps   _____

☐ Tubing   _____

☐ Connections   _____

☐ Airstones   _____

☐ Skimmers, etc.   _____

☐ Lighting   _____

Restock (food, treatments, equipment, etc.):

_____

_____

Additional Notes:

Date: _____ Tank name/ID: _____

Data

Water level: _____ Ammonia level: _____

Temperature: _____ Nitrite level: _____

pH level: _____ Nitrate level: _____

Alkalinity: _____ Salinity: _____

Calcium level: _____ Phosphate level: _____

Iodine level: _____ Magnesium level: _____

Cleaning checklist

Water change? ☐ yes ☐ no   Amount changed: _____

☐ Glass   ☐ Gravel   ☐ Top   ☐ Other _____

Maintenance Checklist

notes

☐ Filters ☐ rinse ☐ replace _____

☐ Pumps _____

☐ Tubing _____

☐ Connections _____

☐ Airstones _____

☐ Skimmers, etc. _____

☐ Lighting _____

Restock (food, treatments, equipment, etc.):

_____

_____

Additional Notes:

Date: _____   Tank name/ID: _____

Data

Water level:	_____	Ammonia level:	_____
Temperature:	_____	Nitrite level:	_____
pH level:	_____	Nitrate level:	_____
Alkalinity:	_____	Salinity:	_____
Calcium level:	_____	Phosphate level:	_____
Iodine level:	_____	Magnesium level:	_____

Cleaning checklist

Water change? ☐ yes ☐ no   Amount changed: _____

☐ Glass   ☐ Gravel   ☐ Top   ☐ Other _____

Maintenance Checklist

notes

☐ Filters   ☐ rinse   ☐ replace   _____
☐ Pumps   _____
☐ Tubing   _____
☐ Connections   _____
☐ Airstones   _____
☐ Skimmers, etc.   _____
☐ Lighting   _____

Restock (food, treatments, equipment, etc.):

_____
_____

Additional Notes:

Date: _____ Tank name/ID: _____

Data

Water level: _____ Ammonia level: _____

Temperature: _____ Nitrite level: _____

pH level: _____ Nitrate level: _____

Alkalinity: _____ Salinity: _____

Calcium level: _____ Phosphate level: _____

Iodine level: _____ Magnesium level: _____

Cleaning checklist

Water change? ☐ yes ☐ no   Amount changed: _____

☐ Glass   ☐ Gravel   ☐ Top   ☐ Other _____

Maintenance Checklist

notes

☐ Filters   ☐ rinse   ☐ replace   _____

☐ Pumps   _____

☐ Tubing   _____

☐ Connections   _____

☐ Airstones   _____

☐ Skimmers, etc.   _____

☐ Lighting   _____

Restock (food, treatments, equipment, etc.):

_____

_____

Additional Notes:

Date: _____   Tank name/ID: _____

Data

Water level:	_____	Ammonia level:	_____
Temperature:	_____	Nitrite level:	_____
pH level:	_____	Nitrate level:	_____
Alkalinity:	_____	Salinity:	_____
Calcium level:	_____	Phosphate level:	_____
Iodine level:	_____	Magnesium level:	_____

Cleaning checklist

Water change? ☐ yes ☐ no   Amount changed: _____

☐ Glass   ☐ Gravel   ☐ Top   ☐ Other _____

Maintenance Checklist

notes

☐ Filters   ☐ rinse   ☐ replace   _____
☐ Pumps   _____
☐ Tubing   _____
☐ Connections   _____
☐ Airstones   _____
☐ Skimmers, etc.   _____
☐ Lighting   _____

Restock (food, treatments, equipment, etc.):

_____
_____

Additional Notes:

Date: _____   Tank name/ID: _____

Data

Water level:	_____	Ammonia level:	_____
Temperature:	_____	Nitrite level:	_____
pH level:	_____	Nitrate level:	_____
Alkalinity:	_____	Salinity:	_____
Calcium level:	_____	Phosphate level:	_____
Iodine level:	_____	Magnesium level:	_____

Cleaning checklist

Water change? ☐ yes ☐ no   Amount changed: _____

☐ Glass   ☐ Gravel   ☐ Top   ☐ Other _____

Maintenance Checklist

notes

☐ Filters   ☐ rinse   ☐ replace   _____
☐ Pumps   _____
☐ Tubing   _____
☐ Connections   _____
☐ Airstones   _____
☐ Skimmers, etc.   _____
☐ Lighting   _____

Restock (food, treatments, equipment, etc.):

_____

_____

Additional Notes:

Date: _____ Tank name/ID: _____

Data

Water level:	_____	Ammonia level:	_____
Temperature:	_____	Nitrite level:	_____
pH level:	_____	Nitrate level:	_____
Alkalinity:	_____	Salinity:	_____
Calcium level:	_____	Phosphate level:	_____
Iodine level:	_____	Magnesium level:	_____

Cleaning checklist

Water change? ☐ yes ☐ no   Amount changed: _____

☐ Glass   ☐ Gravel   ☐ Top   ☐ Other _____

Maintenance Checklist

notes

☐ Filters   ☐ rinse   ☐ replace   _____

☐ Pumps   _____

☐ Tubing   _____

☐ Connections   _____

☐ Airstones   _____

☐ Skimmers, etc.   _____

☐ Lighting   _____

Restock (food, treatments, equipment, etc.):

_____

_____

Additional Notes:

Date: _____ Tank name/ID: _____

Data

Water level:	_____	Ammonia level:	_____
Temperature:	_____	Nitrite level:	_____
pH level:	_____	Nitrate level:	_____
Alkalinity:	_____	Salinity:	_____
Calcium level:	_____	Phosphate level:	_____
Iodine level:	_____	Magnesium level:	_____

Cleaning checklist

Water change? ☐ yes ☐ no   Amount changed: _____

☐ Glass   ☐ Gravel   ☐ Top   ☐ Other _____

Maintenance Checklist

notes

☐ Filters   ☐ rinse   ☐ replace   _____

☐ Pumps   _____

☐ Tubing   _____

☐ Connections   _____

☐ Airstones   _____

☐ Skimmers, etc.   _____

☐ Lighting   _____

Restock (food, treatments, equipment, etc.):

_____

_____

Additional Notes:

Date: Tank name/ID:

Data

Water level:	_____	Ammonia level:	_____
Temperature:	_____	Nitrite level:	_____
pH level:	_____	Nitrate level:	_____
Alkalinity:	_____	Salinity:	_____
Calcium level:	_____	Phosphate level:	_____
Iodine level:	_____	Magnesium level:	_____

Cleaning checklist

Water change? ☐ yes ☐ no   Amount changed: _____

☐ Glass   ☐ Gravel   ☐ Top   ☐ Other _____

Maintenance Checklist

notes

☐ Filters   ☐ rinse   ☐ replace   _____

☐ Pumps   _____

☐ Tubing   _____

☐ Connections   _____

☐ Airstones   _____

☐ Skimmers, etc.   _____

☐ Lighting   _____

Restock (food, treatments, equipment, etc.):

_____

_____

Additional Notes:

Date: _____ Tank name/ID: _____

Data

Water level:	_____	Ammonia level:	_____
Temperature:	_____	Nitrite level:	_____
pH level:	_____	Nitrate level:	_____
Alkalinity:	_____	Salinity:	_____
Calcium level:	_____	Phosphate level:	_____
Iodine level:	_____	Magnesium level:	_____

Cleaning checklist

Water change? ☐ yes ☐ no   Amount changed: _____

☐ Glass   ☐ Gravel   ☐ Top   ☐ Other _____

Maintenance Checklist

notes

☐ Filters   ☐ rinse   ☐ replace   _____
☐ Pumps   _____
☐ Tubing   _____
☐ Connections   _____
☐ Airstones   _____
☐ Skimmers, etc.   _____
☐ Lighting   _____

Restock (food, treatments, equipment, etc.):

_____

_____

Additional Notes:

Date: Tank name/ID:

Data

Water level: _____   Ammonia level: _____

Temperature: _____   Nitrite level: _____

pH level: _____   Nitrate level: _____

Alkalinity: _____   Salinity: _____

Calcium level: _____   Phosphate level: _____

Iodine level: _____   Magnesium level: _____

Cleaning checklist

Water change? ☐ yes ☐ no   Amount changed: _____

☐ Glass   ☐ Gravel   ☐ Top   ☐ Other _____

Maintenance Checklist

<u>notes</u>

☐ Filters   ☐ rinse   ☐ replace   _____

☐ Pumps   _____

☐ Tubing   _____

☐ Connections   _____

☐ Airstones   _____

☐ Skimmers, etc.   _____

☐ Lighting   _____

Restock (food, treatments, equipment, etc.):

_____

_____

Additional Notes:

Date: Tank name/ID:

Data

Water level:	_____	Ammonia level:	_____
Temperature:	_____	Nitrite level:	_____
pH level:	_____	Nitrate level:	_____
Alkalinity:	_____	Salinity:	_____
Calcium level:	_____	Phosphate level:	_____
Iodine level:	_____	Magnesium level:	_____

Cleaning checklist

Water change? ☐ yes ☐ no   Amount changed: _____

☐ Glass   ☐ Gravel   ☐ Top   ☐ Other _____

Maintenance Checklist

notes

☐ Filters   ☐ rinse   ☐ replace   _____
☐ Pumps   _____
☐ Tubing   _____
☐ Connections   _____
☐ Airstones   _____
☐ Skimmers, etc.   _____
☐ Lighting   _____

Restock (food, treatments, equipment, etc.):

_____
_____

Additional Notes:

Date: Tank name/ID:

Data

Water level:	_____	Ammonia level:	_____
Temperature:	_____	Nitrite level:	_____
pH level:	_____	Nitrate level:	_____
Alkalinity:	_____	Salinity:	_____
Calcium level:	_____	Phosphate level:	_____
Iodine level:	_____	Magnesium level:	_____

Cleaning checklist

Water change? ☐ yes ☐ no   Amount changed: _____

☐ Glass   ☐ Gravel   ☐ Top   ☐ Other _____

Maintenance Checklist

notes

☐ Filters   ☐ rinse   ☐ replace   _____

☐ Pumps   _____

☐ Tubing   _____

☐ Connections   _____

☐ Airstones   _____

☐ Skimmers, etc.   _____

☐ Lighting   _____

Restock (food, treatments, equipment, etc.):

_____

_____

Additional Notes:

Date: Tank name/ID:

Data

Water level:	_____	Ammonia level:	_____
Temperature:	_____	Nitrite level:	_____
pH level:	_____	Nitrate level:	_____
Alkalinity:	_____	Salinity:	_____
Calcium level:	_____	Phosphate level:	_____
Iodine level:	_____	Magnesium level:	_____

Cleaning checklist

Water change? ☐ yes ☐ no   Amount changed: _____

☐ Glass   ☐ Gravel   ☐ Top   ☐ Other _____

Maintenance Checklist

notes

☐ Filters   ☐ rinse   ☐ replace   _____

☐ Pumps   _____

☐ Tubing   _____

☐ Connections   _____

☐ Airstones   _____

☐ Skimmers, etc.   _____

☐ Lighting   _____

Restock (food, treatments, equipment, etc.):

_____

_____

Additional Notes:

Date: Tank name/ID:

Data

Water level:	_____	Ammonia level:	_____
Temperature:	_____	Nitrite level:	_____
pH level:	_____	Nitrate level:	_____
Alkalinity:	_____	Salinity:	_____
Calcium level:	_____	Phosphate level:	_____
Iodine level:	_____	Magnesium level:	_____

Cleaning checklist

Water change? ☐ yes ☐ no   Amount changed: _____

☐ Glass   ☐ Gravel   ☐ Top   ☐ Other _____

Maintenance Checklist

<u>notes</u>

☐ Filters   ☐ rinse   ☐ replace   _____

☐ Pumps   _____

☐ Tubing   _____

☐ Connections   _____

☐ Airstones   _____

☐ Skimmers, etc.   _____

☐ Lighting   _____

Restock (food, treatments, equipment, etc.):

_____

_____

Additional Notes:

Date: Tank name/ID:

Data

Water level:	_____	Ammonia level:	_____
Temperature:	_____	Nitrite level:	_____
pH level:	_____	Nitrate level:	_____
Alkalinity:	_____	Salinity:	_____
Calcium level:	_____	Phosphate level:	_____
Iodine level:	_____	Magnesium level:	_____

Cleaning checklist

Water change? ☐ yes ☐ no   Amount changed: _____

☐ Glass   ☐ Gravel   ☐ Top   ☐ Other _____

Maintenance Checklist

notes

☐ Filters   ☐ rinse   ☐ replace   _____

☐ Pumps   _____

☐ Tubing   _____

☐ Connections   _____

☐ Airstones   _____

☐ Skimmers, etc.   _____

☐ Lighting   _____

Restock (food, treatments, equipment, etc.):

_____
_____

Additional Notes:

Date: _____ Tank name/ID: _____

Data

Water level: _____ Ammonia level: _____

Temperature: _____ Nitrite level: _____

pH level: _____ Nitrate level: _____

Alkalinity: _____ Salinity: _____

Calcium level: _____ Phosphate level: _____

Iodine level: _____ Magnesium level: _____

Cleaning checklist

Water change? ☐ yes ☐ no   Amount changed: _____

☐ Glass   ☐ Gravel   ☐ Top   ☐ Other _____

Maintenance Checklist

notes

☐ Filters   ☐ rinse   ☐ replace   _____

☐ Pumps   _____

☐ Tubing   _____

☐ Connections   _____

☐ Airstones   _____

☐ Skimmers, etc.   _____

☐ Lighting   _____

Restock (food, treatments, equipment, etc.):

_____

_____

Additional Notes:

Date: _____   Tank name/ID: _____

Data

Water level:	_____	Ammonia level:	_____
Temperature:	_____	Nitrite level:	_____
pH level:	_____	Nitrate level:	_____
Alkalinity:	_____	Salinity:	_____
Calcium level:	_____	Phosphate level:	_____
Iodine level:	_____	Magnesium level:	_____

Cleaning checklist

Water change? ☐ yes ☐ no   Amount changed: _____

☐ Glass   ☐ Gravel   ☐ Top   ☐ Other _____

Maintenance Checklist

notes

☐ Filters   ☐ rinse   ☐ replace   _____
☐ Pumps   _____
☐ Tubing   _____
☐ Connections   _____
☐ Airstones   _____
☐ Skimmers, etc.   _____
☐ Lighting   _____

Restock (food, treatments, equipment, etc.):

_____

_____

Additional Notes:

Date: Tank name/ID:

Data

Water level:	_____	Ammonia level:	_____
Temperature:	_____	Nitrite level:	_____
pH level:	_____	Nitrate level:	_____
Alkalinity:	_____	Salinity:	_____
Calcium level:	_____	Phosphate level:	_____
Iodine level:	_____	Magnesium level:	_____

Cleaning checklist

Water change? ☐ yes ☐ no   Amount changed: _____

☐ Glass   ☐ Gravel   ☐ Top   ☐ Other _____

Maintenance Checklist

<u>notes</u>

☐ Filters   ☐ rinse   ☐ replace   _____

☐ Pumps   _____

☐ Tubing   _____

☐ Connections   _____

☐ Airstones   _____

☐ Skimmers, etc.   _____

☐ Lighting   _____

Restock (food, treatments, equipment, etc.):

_____

_____

Additional Notes:

Date: Tank name/ID:

Data

Water level:	_____	Ammonia level:	_____
Temperature:	_____	Nitrite level:	_____
pH level:	_____	Nitrate level:	_____
Alkalinity:	_____	Salinity:	_____
Calcium level:	_____	Phosphate level:	_____
Iodine level:	_____	Magnesium level:	_____

Cleaning checklist

Water change? ☐ yes ☐ no   Amount changed: _____

☐ Glass   ☐ Gravel   ☐ Top   ☐ Other _____

Maintenance Checklist

<u>notes</u>

☐ Filters   ☐ rinse   ☐ replace   _____

☐ Pumps   _____

☐ Tubing   _____

☐ Connections   _____

☐ Airstones   _____

☐ Skimmers, etc.   _____

☐ Lighting   _____

Restock (food, treatments, equipment, etc.):

_____

_____

Additional Notes:

Date: Tank name/ID:

Data

Water level:	_____	Ammonia level:	_____
Temperature:	_____	Nitrite level:	_____
pH level:	_____	Nitrate level:	_____
Alkalinity:	_____	Salinity:	_____
Calcium level:	_____	Phosphate level:	_____
Iodine level:	_____	Magnesium level:	_____

Cleaning checklist

Water change? ☐ yes ☐ no   Amount changed: _____

☐ Glass   ☐ Gravel   ☐ Top   ☐ Other _____

Maintenance Checklist

notes

☐ Filters   ☐ rinse   ☐ replace   _____

☐ Pumps   _____

☐ Tubing   _____

☐ Connections   _____

☐ Airstones   _____

☐ Skimmers, etc.   _____

☐ Lighting   _____

Restock (food, treatments, equipment, etc.):

_____

_____

Additional Notes:

Date: Tank name/ID:

Data

Water level:	_____	Ammonia level:	_____
Temperature:	_____	Nitrite level:	_____
pH level:	_____	Nitrate level:	_____
Alkalinity:	_____	Salinity:	_____
Calcium level:	_____	Phosphate level:	_____
Iodine level:	_____	Magnesium level:	_____

Cleaning checklist

Water change? ☐ yes ☐ no   Amount changed: _____

☐ Glass   ☐ Gravel   ☐ Top   ☐ Other _____

Maintenance Checklist

notes

☐ Filters   ☐ rinse   ☐ replace   _____

☐ Pumps   _____

☐ Tubing   _____

☐ Connections   _____

☐ Airstones   _____

☐ Skimmers, etc.   _____

☐ Lighting   _____

Restock (food, treatments, equipment, etc.):

_____

_____

Additional Notes:

Date: Tank name/ID:

Data

Water level: _____   Ammonia level: _____

Temperature: _____   Nitrite level: _____

pH level: _____   Nitrate level: _____

Alkalinity: _____   Salinity: _____

Calcium level: _____   Phosphate level: _____

Iodine level: _____   Magnesium level: _____

Cleaning checklist

Water change? ☐ yes ☐ no   Amount changed: _____

☐ Glass   ☐ Gravel   ☐ Top   ☐ Other _____

Maintenance Checklist

notes

☐ Filters   ☐ rinse   ☐ replace   _____
☐ Pumps   _____
☐ Tubing   _____
☐ Connections   _____
☐ Airstones   _____
☐ Skimmers, etc.   _____
☐ Lighting   _____

Restock (food, treatments, equipment, etc.):
_____
_____

Additional Notes:

Date: Tank name/ID:

Data

Water level:	_____	Ammonia level:		_____
Temperature:	_____	Nitrite level:		_____
pH level:	_____	Nitrate level:		_____
Alkalinity:	_____	Salinity:		_____
Calcium level:	_____	Phosphate level:		_____
Iodine level:	_____	Magnesium level:		_____

Cleaning checklist

Water change? ☐ yes ☐ no   Amount changed: _____

☐ Glass   ☐ Gravel   ☐ Top   ☐ Other _____

Maintenance Checklist

<u>notes</u>

☐ Filters ☐ rinse ☐ replace _____

☐ Pumps _____

☐ Tubing _____

☐ Connections _____

☐ Airstones _____

☐ Skimmers, etc. _____

☐ Lighting _____

Restock (food, treatments, equipment, etc.):

_____

_____

Additional Notes:

Date: Tank name/ID:

Data

Water level:	_____	Ammonia level:	_____
Temperature:	_____	Nitrite level:	_____
pH level:	_____	Nitrate level:	_____
Alkalinity:	_____	Salinity:	_____
Calcium level:	_____	Phosphate level:	_____
Iodine level:	_____	Magnesium level:	_____

Cleaning checklist

Water change? ☐ yes ☐ no   Amount changed: _____

☐ Glass   ☐ Gravel   ☐ Top   ☐ Other _____

Maintenance Checklist

notes

☐ Filters   ☐ rinse   ☐ replace   _____

☐ Pumps   _____

☐ Tubing   _____

☐ Connections _____

☐ Airstones   _____

☐ Skimmers, etc. _____

☐ Lighting   _____

Restock (food, treatments, equipment, etc.):

_____

_____

Additional Notes:

Date: Tank name/ID:

Data

Water level:	_____	Ammonia level:	_____
Temperature:	_____	Nitrite level:	_____
pH level:	_____	Nitrate level:	_____
Alkalinity:	_____	Salinity:	_____
Calcium level:	_____	Phosphate level:	_____
Iodine level:	_____	Magnesium level:	_____

Cleaning checklist

Water change? ☐ yes ☐ no   Amount changed: _____

☐ Glass   ☐ Gravel   ☐ Top   ☐ Other _____

Maintenance Checklist

notes

☐ Filters   ☐ rinse   ☐ replace   _____

☐ Pumps   _____

☐ Tubing   _____

☐ Connections   _____

☐ Airstones   _____

☐ Skimmers, etc.   _____

☐ Lighting   _____

Restock (food, treatments, equipment, etc.):

_____

_____

Additional Notes:

Date: Tank name/ID:

Data

Water level: _____   Ammonia level: _____

Temperature: _____   Nitrite level: _____

pH level: _____   Nitrate level: _____

Alkalinity: _____   Salinity: _____

Calcium level: _____   Phosphate level: _____

Iodine level: _____   Magnesium level: _____

Cleaning checklist

Water change? ☐ yes ☐ no   Amount changed: _____

☐ Glass   ☐ Gravel   ☐ Top   ☐ Other _____

Maintenance Checklist

notes

☐ Filters   ☐ rinse   ☐ replace   _____

☐ Pumps   _____

☐ Tubing   _____

☐ Connections   _____

☐ Airstones   _____

☐ Skimmers, etc.   _____

☐ Lighting   _____

Restock (food, treatments, equipment, etc.):

_____

_____

Additional Notes:

Date: Tank name/ID:

Data

Water level: _____   Ammonia level: _____

Temperature: _____   Nitrite level: _____

pH level: _____   Nitrate level: _____

Alkalinity: _____   Salinity: _____

Calcium level: _____   Phosphate level: _____

Iodine level: _____   Magnesium level: _____

Cleaning checklist

Water change?   ☐ yes   ☐ no   Amount changed: _____

☐ Glass   ☐ Gravel   ☐ Top   ☐ Other _____

Maintenance Checklist

<u>notes</u>

☐ Filters   ☐ rinse   ☐ replace   _____

☐ Pumps   _____

☐ Tubing   _____

☐ Connections   _____

☐ Airstones   _____

☐ Skimmers, etc.   _____

☐ Lighting   _____

Restock (food, treatments, equipment, etc.):

_____

_____

Additional Notes:

Date: Tank name/ID:

Data

Water level: _____   Ammonia level: _____

Temperature: _____   Nitrite level: _____

pH level: _____   Nitrate level: _____

Alkalinity: _____   Salinity: _____

Calcium level: _____   Phosphate level: _____

Iodine level: _____   Magnesium level: _____

Cleaning checklist

Water change? ☐ yes ☐ no   Amount changed: _____

☐ Glass   ☐ Gravel   ☐ Top   ☐ Other _____

Maintenance Checklist

<u>notes</u>

☐ Filters   ☐ rinse   ☐ replace   _____

☐ Pumps   _____

☐ Tubing   _____

☐ Connections   _____

☐ Airstones   _____

☐ Skimmers, etc.   _____

☐ Lighting   _____

Restock (food, treatments, equipment, etc.):

_____

_____

Additional Notes:

Date: Tank name/ID:

Data

Water level: _____   Ammonia level: _____

Temperature: _____   Nitrite level: _____

pH level: _____   Nitrate level: _____

Alkalinity: _____   Salinity: _____

Calcium level: _____   Phosphate level: _____

Iodine level: _____   Magnesium level: _____

Cleaning checklist

Water change? ☐ yes ☐ no   Amount changed: _____

☐ Glass   ☐ Gravel   ☐ Top   ☐ Other _____

Maintenance Checklist

notes

☐ Filters   ☐ rinse   ☐ replace   _____

☐ Pumps   _____

☐ Tubing   _____

☐ Connections   _____

☐ Airstones   _____

☐ Skimmers, etc.   _____

☐ Lighting   _____

Restock (food, treatments, equipment, etc.):

_____

_____

Additional Notes:

Made in the USA
Las Vegas, NV
23 December 2023

83476880R00171